TESTED METHODS IN TOWN AND COUNTRY CHURCHES

BY

EDMUND DeS. BRUNNER

With a Foreword by
HONORABLE GIFFORD PINCHOT
GOVERNOR OF PENNSYLVANIA

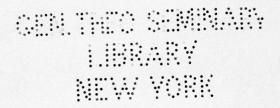

NEW YORK
GEORGE H. DORAN COMPANY

COPYRIGHT, 1923,
BY GEORGE H. DORAN COMPANY

TESTED METHODS IN TOWN AND COUNTRY CHURCHES. I

PRINTED IN THE UNITED STATES OF AMERICA

FOREWORD

By Honorable Gifford Pinchot

GOVERNOR OF PENNSYLVANIA

In 1909 it was my privilege to serve as a member of the Country Life Commission set up by President Roosevelt. At that time if somebody had prophesied that only fourteen years later a volume would be published giving, as this one does, not the *theory* of a successful ministry in the country church but actual concrete methods employed in forty country churches which had won conspicuous success through the use of these methods, I should probably have thought the prophecy entirely too optimistic.

I remember a phrase in the recommendations made by President Roosevelt's Commission which bears very specifically upon the subject of this volume: "The country church of the future is to be held responsible for the great ideals of community life as well as of personal character." Just because the Commission felt that the country church was not serving, as in the earlier periods of our history, to promote the social and religious well-being of the country, it stressed the social obligations of the rural church.

The present volume shows that country churches succeed by living up to principles which the report recommended. They have been the servants, not only to their constituents, but to whole communities. They have been social centers in the best sense and at the same time have remained true to their distinctive evangelistic purpose. In a word, they have demonstrated that the church which fully represents Jesus Christ ministers to all sides of community life, and must supply the motive for many of its purely social activities.

As one, who, in company with Mr. Charles O. Gill, has

had practical experience in the work of making rural religious surveys, I have followed with profound interest and satisfaction the studies of the church in rural America which have been completed by the Committee on Social and Religious Surveys. It seems eminently fitting that the careful investigation made by Dr. Brunner and his colleagues, as published in the twelve volumes of the Committee's Town and Country Series, should be followed by this study of the country church at its best. It shows how others have met and overcome the very difficulties which the average rural church is facing. I can imagine no better inspiration for the rural pastor than the reading of this book and its companion volume, "Churches of Distinction in Town and Country"—and only those who are familiar with the difficult problems which the country pastor faces can realize his need of inspiration.

INTRODUCTION

The Committee on Social and Religious Surveys conducted during the year 1922 an investigation of the most successful town and country churches of Protestant persuasion that it could find anywhere in the United States. The study was undertaken in order that the experience of these churches might be available to all other churches similarly placed.

For the purposes of this study no attempt was made to arrive inductively at a scientific definition of what constitutes a "successful" church. The test of a church's "success" most generally accepted by the denominational boards consulted in the preliminaries of the study is the service, spiritual and material, which it renders to the community of which it is a part and the measure of support which in turn it receives from the community. This test was accepted as the basis of the present investigation.

Two books have resulted from the investigation; a volume made up of stories of certain of the individual churches, which has been published under the title of "Churches of Distinction in Town and Country," and this one, which describes the methods employed by those churches. The present volume is intended for use in theological seminaries, in graduate summer schools for the training of town and country ministers, by classes in leadership-training within congregations, and above all by individual town or country pastors at work in their fields. Both form and content of the volume have been adapted so far as possible to meet the wishes of officials of home mission boards who have had these purposes in mind.

TYPES OF COMMUNITIES STUDIED

To make sure that the investigation would cover the greatest possible number of churches differently placed in respect to environment, the Committee on Social and Religious Surveys, aided by the findings of its previous studies and by the advice of rural sociologists specially consulted, drew up a list of town and country communities of twenty different types. It was believed that among these types every area in the United States would be represented. The communities, arranged in accordance with the plan of regional distribution used in other surveys by this Committee, follow:

Northern Colonial Area

1. A Scotch-Irish community, general farming background, preferably an open country church.
2. A German community, probably in Pennsylania, general farming and open country or small village church, one of the liturgical group.
3. New England communities, villages, illustrating:
    a—A denominational community church in command of the field by comity agreement.
    b—A federated church.
    c—An interdenominational or union church.
4. New York village or town of 1,500 to 5,000 population with developing industrial interest, some foreign element but farm connections still existing.

Middle West and Prairie

5. Village in wheat belt where there is migrant labor affected by church, preferably in Kansas or Nebraska.
6. County seat, Middle West, several denominations represented, having program of community coöperation, preferably a town with considerable retired farmer element.
7. Same social and economic background as "6" above, but in which one church is forging ahead regardless of competition.

Northwest

8. Scandinavian community, dairy or grain region in Minnesota or North Dakota, preferably a church with a developed educational program and an advanced economic program.

South

9. Good average open country community in cotton belt.
10. Cotton mill town.
11. Southern mountain community with or without any industrial development but in which outside aid has affected progress, especially along educational, other cultural or health lines.
12. Negro community in cotton section, either village or open country.

Southwest or Pacific

13. Mexican community with Protestant church, either a small industrial or a farming community or a combination of both.
14. Indian community in Southwest, illustrating transition from nomadic tribal to settled agricultural life.
15. Community in irrigated country, trucking or small fruit, large influx of foreign seasonal labor affected by adequate church program.
16. Lumber or mining town with foreign element.

Range

17. Town in cattle-raising or dry-farming district in which church is doing significant larger parish work.

General

18. Czechoslovak community in the Middle West or in Texas, general farming background, open country or small village church.
19. Rural industrial village, preferably with polyglot foreign population.
20. Community, industrial or farming, with large permanent element of later (southern European) immigration in which English-speaking church is doing significant work in reaching foreign born.

No churches were discovered for a few of these types. More than one church was selected in each of the more important of these groups.

Denominational leaders, state and national, and state leaders in agriculture and education, were then asked to name, in communities of the various kinds, churches doing successful work. Investigation was also made of the files of the Interchurch World Movement surveys and of religious periodicals. From this study and inquiry resulted a list of nearly 700 churches. After preliminary investigation half of these churches were eliminated. The Committee sent to representatives of each of the others a statement as to the nature of the investigation; a request for permission to have one or more of its workers study the church in case the committee should so elect; and a questionnaire.

Responses were received from more than 90 per cent. of the ministers and other leaders addressed. On the basis of these replies the Committee selected forty churches. In making the choice, there was an attempt to include a wide range of denominations and of types of work. If two churches illustrated a given situation equally well, preference was given to the church of the denomination having the fewer representatives on the list. No effort was made to specialize in village churches rather than in town churches, or in country churches in preference to town and village churches. The Committee endeavored, instead, to choose successful churches which, taken together, would represent every kind of community.

METHOD OF INVESTIGATION

Each of the churches selected was subjected to careful investigation by competent field workers during a period lasting from eight days to a month, in the spring, summer or fall of 1922.

In every instance the churches studied gave full coöperation. Pastors, church officers, and members were untiring in their efforts to obtain all the information desired, and contributed in the aggregate many days of valuable time.

SIGNIFICANCE OF MATERIAL

The significant thing is that what is here presented is not theory but the actual practice of churches that are successful.

From the experience of these churches, it is believed, the country church of America has much to learn.

This volume is submitted with a word of caution. It is a composite account of forty churches, and therefore contains a multiplicity of suggestive detail. No one church can do all the things of which it tells. Few can do any one thing in exactly the way here indicated. An outstanding tendency of the churches investigated was found to be adaptation of program to need, or method to situation. Their practice must likewise be adapted to varying local conditions.

WHAT OF THE CHURCHES?

For a still better understanding of the methods of work described in this book, an analysis of the situation of these churches as it existed at the time of the survey will be found valuable. These churches are not situated in unusual, above-the-average communities which have now ordered their religious life so that but one church serves all elements of the population. Furthermore, most of these churches began their development when at just an average level of efficiency and success, while many began at a level considerably below the average. The success they have won has come because of the consecration of their leaders, because of the methods they have developed and because they have applied those methods with unceasing effort. They have traveled no easy road to distinction.

DISTRIBUTION OF CHURCHES

Six of them are town churches, twenty-two are in villages, and twelve are in the open country. Of the villages, seven have less than 500 population. Some of the churches have from eight to thirteen different denominational bodies represented in their present membership.

Four of the organizations studied are federated churches made up of what were formerly separate congregations differing in denomination. One is an undenominational community church. Ten of the churches are the only ones in their communities, either because of federation or of the withdrawal of some other denomination by agreement, or because they alone survived. Two more share their fields with only very small churches of the Holy Roller type. The church at Parma shows excellently how wide an appeal a church may have. It successfully reaches all. In its active membership are former members of sixteen different denominations, including such diverse groups as Methodists, Lutherans, Congregationalists, Roman Catholics, Nazarenes and Latter Day Saints.

EXTENT OF PARISH

Virtually all of these churches include people from both village and country. Even those in the larger towns draw considerably from the countryside and have broken down such barriers as often exist between town and country. Grace Church at Spencer, Iowa, draws 20 per cent. of its 900 members from rural areas surrounding the town.

The open country membership exceeds that of the village or town in eight of the thirty-two churches located in non-industrial towns or villages. In ten others the proportion ranges from one-third to 90 per cent. In most other instances from one-sixth to one-fourth of the membership is drawn from the surrounding countryside. In the entire group of churches, less than half the members live within a mile of the church building. A fifth live from two to five miles from the church and nearly a fifth live more than five miles away. This long-range influence is not accidental. The churches accept full responsibility for the care of the communities in which they are. They not only care for members at the outer edge of their parishes, but systematically cover, with their evangelistic and social programs, the whole territory for which they are responsible.

Seven out of every ten of these churches have extended their parish boundaries until they are coterminus, or nearly so, with the boundaries of the community. In a few instances the parishes extend beyond the community boundaries. The parish boundaries of only a fifth are markedly smaller than those of the communities, and in each of these cases the church is either reaching only one neighborhood in the community or is meeting exceptionally strong competition. This is an unusually good record. The Interchurch World Movement surveys found that the church was rare indeed whose parish boundaries included the whole community.

Whatever their past, most of these churches are now larger and stronger than the average. Only nine have fewer than 100 members, and in most cases they are the churches in very small communities or in communities in which there is a considerable proportion of Roman Catholic population. Nearly half the churches fall within the next membership group of between 100 and 200. This group also has the most extended activities. Six more churches have between 200 and 300 members and a final six range from 349 to nearly 1,100. Three of the last six are in county seats that have populations of from 2,590 to nearly 5,000. These three, however, share the field in each instance with half a dozen or more churches. Of the other large churches, the largest is in a village of 750 inhabitants which draws heavily from the surrounding countryside; another is an open country church with 507 members; and a third is the community church in a village of 600 people. It has 349 resident members.

The attendance in these churches is quite remarkable. Six of them average more than 200 at the morning service; three of these have more than 450 and one more than 800. Often people have to go early to get seats in the main auditorium. For the whole group the morning attendance averages 70 per cent. of the resident membership, and the evening attendance 52 per cent. At least one representative of 75 per cent. of the families on the rolls of these churches is in regular attendance at least one service every Sunday.

In six of the churches, which make up 15 per cent. of the entire number, the average attendance at either the morning service or the evening service, or at both services, exceeds the resident membership. The audiences are well distributed among the various age- and sex-groups. At the morning service 39 per cent. are adult women; 31 per cent. adult men; 23 per cent. are members under twenty-one years of age, and the remainder are children. In the evening, adult men and women in equal proportion make up three-fifths of the audiences. With the exception of a few small children, young people make up the rest of the congregations.

The men at the morning services in twelve of the churches equal or exceed the women in number; while in eight the proportion of young people exceeds that of any other group. In the evening the proportion of men equals or exceeds that of women in fifteen churches. In an equal number, the young people have more representatives than any of the other groups.

AGE AND SEX OF MEMBERS

For the purposes of this study the membership of these churches has been divided into three groups, including respectively persons under twenty-one, those between twenty-one and forty-five, and those forty-six or older. It was found that nearly a fourth of the members were under twenty-one and that exactly two-thirds were under forty-five years of age. In some cases more than a third of the members on the roll were under twenty-one years of age. This was owing in part to the fact that some of the churches are in communities still so young that few people have had time to grow old. Another explanation is the great attractiveness to the young people of the virile programs undertaken by these churches. The older congregations include persons of all ages and the churches minister to all of them successfully. In them there are many pews in which representatives of three generations sit together. Slightly more than three-fifths of the present membership of these churches joined within the last decade. The rest of the membership is almost equally divided between those who joined between ten and twenty years ago and those who united with the church in the more distant past.

These churches also reach both sex-groups. In the whole list there is but one "woman's" church. In the others, male members constitute anywhere from a third to three-fifths of the total membership.

OCCUPATION OF MEMBERS

More than 40 per cent. of the members are gainfully employed. Thirty-six per cent. of these are farmers who own their farms, while 12 per cent. are farm-renters, and another 12 per cent. are professional people. Thirteen per cent. are in business. Seven per cent. are farm-laborers. Of the other scattering occupations, clerks of various kinds form the predominant group.

FACTS REGARDING ORGANIZATIONS

In the Sunday schools there is no predominant age-group other than the adult. The proportion of the total membership varies little for the different age groupings up to twenty years. Almost 20 per cent. more of males than of females on the church roll belong to the Sunday school. Sixty per cent. of the entire membership of these churches is enrolled in some one of the subsidiary organizations. In this respect the young people's group makes the best showing, with 80 per cent. enrolled. The total number of males so interested is 55 per cent. and of females 63 per cent.

LENGTH OF SUCCESS

The average period over which these churches have been succeeding is seven years. But two entirely different types of churches figure in this average. The first type includes such churches as Stanton, Middle Octoraro and Dayton, which have behind them years of tradition. These are among the eighteen which exceed the average of seven years. For the other twenty-two, the periods of success have covered a shorter period. The average is 3.2 years.

MINISTERS

The ministers of these churches are not different from ministers everywhere, save that a large proportion are men with college and seminary training. Twenty-five have had the advantages of both college and seminary. A dozen others are college men and the other three are seminary trained only. If they differ from other ministers in anything it is in their capacity for ceaseless work. This is the price of their success. Otherwise—in temperament, in age, in person, and in methods of leadership—they are as unlike as men of any other group could be. Had they all been of one general type, it might have been fair to conclude that men of that type possess those general qualities of leadership essential in successful church organizations. This, however, is not the case. The clue to the success of these churches does not lie in their employing a distinctive type of minister. The pastorates, however, are longer than the average. The average length of time that each of these ministers has been with his present congregation is in excess of four and one-half years, whereas the average total pastorate of the churches in the twenty-five counties studied by the Committee on Social and Religious Surveys was 3.8 years.

These churches, then, have been selected as representative of a considerable number which have won more than local distinction. They have been chosen to illustrate rural religious work in various kinds of communities and by various denominations. Growing out of average or below-average situations, and located in communities in no way especially favored, these churches have broadened their scope and influence, have increased their memberships and attendance, have reached and held all age, sex, and occupational groups, and have developed programs that have resulted in achievements far beyond those of the average town and country churches in America. That is why an analysis of their methods holds promise of interest and inspiration.

State	Community	Church	Pastor
Mississippi	Shuford	Shuford Circuit (Methodist Episcopal South)	N. D. Guerry
Missouri	Rolla	First Methodist Episcopal	Claude S. Hanby, Ph.D.
Nebraska	Arnold	Baptist Rural Parish	Perry O. Silvara
"	Gresham	Wayland Christian	C. G. Nelson
New Jersey	New Monmouth	Baptist	A. H. Sutphin
New Mexico	Cimarron	Methodist Episcopal	Gilbert Traveller
New York	Canoga	Presbyterian	G. H. Mickelson
"	Harrisville	Methodist Episcopal	William K. Bradshaw
"	Perry	Brick Presbyterian	Merlyn A. Chappel
Ohio	Garrettsville	United-Baptist, Congregational and Disciples	Payson L. Curtiss
Oklahoma	Roosevelt	Methodist Episcopal	John Thacker
Pennsylvania	Duncannon	Asbury Methodist Episcopal	L. Elbert Wilson
"	Esterly	Schwarzwald Reformed Church in the U. S.	J. Lucian Roush
"	Lander	Methodist Episcopal	Thomas E. Colley
"	Quarryville	Middle Octoraro Presbyterian	George H. Shea
Texas	Gonzales	Gonzales Circuit (Methodist Episcopal)	J. L. Edmondson
Utah	Bingham Canyon	Community Methodist Episcopal	Lester P. Fagen
Wisconsin	Honey Creek	First Baptist	Ralph Berry

CONTENTS

		PAGE
FOREWORD BY HONORABLE GIFFORD PINCHOT	. . .	v
INTRODUCTION		vii
ACKNOWLEDGMENTS		xvii

CHAPTER

I	EVANGELISM	25
II	WORSHIP AND SERVICES	38
III	RELIGIOUS EDUCATION	47
IV	WORK FOR AGE AND SEX GROUPS	66
V	THE PLANT AND ITS EQUIPMENT	89
VI	CHURCH FINANCE	109
VII	ORGANIZING THE CHURCH FOR THE PROGRAM	123
VIII	PUBLICITY	140
IX	COMMUNITY WELFARE AND CHURCH COÖPERA-TION	154
X	MEASURING SUCCESS	165
	INDEX	171

TESTED METHODS IN
TOWN AND COUNTRY CHURCHES

TESTED METHODS IN TOWN AND COUNTRY CHURCHES

Chapter I

EVANGELISM

The forty churches which form the subject of this study both gain members and hold and nurture them. During the year before this study was made a gross gain in membership of 17.3 per cent. was registered, and a net gain of 14 per cent. Moreover these churches are evangelistic. Seventy-one per cent. of their new members came on confession of faith and only 29 per cent. by letter. This is in marked contrast with the showing of the churches of twenty-five typical counties throughout America, studied by the Committee on Social and Religious Surveys, which found the average net gain to be less than 3 per cent.

The reasons for the success of the evangelistic work of these churches are many, but two underlie all the others. In the first place the churches make an appeal that is both broad and basic. They lead men and women to the Christian life. In the second place they practise the gospel they preach. They make their successful appeal to the hearts of men and women because they exemplify so well what they stand for. Evangelism is, therefore, the keystone of their program.

All these churches have one time of the year in which their evangelistic efforts culminate. These efforts are brought to an end in different ways. With some, the culmination is in a series of evangelistic services, sometimes known as a protracted meeting. With others, it is in quiet, personal appeals made at the time of year when the young people declare publicly through the rite of confirmation their allegiance to God and the church.

Various methods are used to prepare for the evangelistic harvest. In a number of the churches a survey is held to be a prerequisite. This survey is on a house-to-house basis and no family is overlooked. Where there are other churches in the community, this study is generally coöperative. Names of persons canvassed are referred to the different churches in accordance with expressed preferences, or with information at hand if there has been no expression of preference. For example, if one man has been known to attend a church occasionally or to seek its service for funeral or a baptism, his name is given to that church for its attention even though he may have placed himself in the non-preference column. These surveys are carried beyond the corporate limits of the community. Consultations have been held with churches of nearby communities and no-man's lands have been discovered. Dividing lines have then been drawn between communities and all unchurched families listed. This has proved very effective.

ENLISTING THE MEMBERSHIP

No evangelistic campaign can succeed without the whole-hearted support of the entire church. The membership is enlisted in various ways. Most churches use several methods simultaneously. Letters are sent to church members; or, as in one church community, "to all the Christian people," announcing the services and asking for definite coöperation. Some outstanding passages in one such letter follow:

There are some things that each of you can do that will mean a great deal to the success of this enterprise for the Master. I take the privilege of enumerating them:
1. You can pray. . . .
2. Be at each meeting YOURSELF. . . .

3. Invite others to come. . . .
4. Talk to others about their relation to God and Jesus Christ. . . .

PRAYER MEETINGS

Cottage prayer meetings almost invariably feature the preparation for an evangelistic campaign. Members in the different parts of the parish gather once a week during a month or more, before the opening of the campaign, to pray and plan for its success. Such meetings can be made fruitful where the pastor and the leaders have definite plans and objectives. The entire membership is not only brought into a state of spiritual expectancy but is instructed regarding the things that need to be done.

TRAINING PERSONAL WORKERS

Nothing is more damaging to an evangelistic campaign than are ill-advised efforts on the part of the members. A person cannot be approached successfully in respect to his relation to things Divine if the approach is made in haphazard fashion. The reason for the appeal that is to be made, the challenge of the church, the obligation and opportunity of fellowship and service—these must be presented with conviction. More than that, their presentation must be influenced by a knowledge of the person to whom they are being presented. Classes for personal workers are therefore important features in preparation for an evangelistic campaign. Frequently they are held in connection with the cottage prayer meetings. Lists of those who are unchurched are gone over and names are assigned both for invitation and for interview. In one church the pastor goes so far as to discuss with his lieutenants the themes of his sermons and upon occasion the lieutenants themselves, after receiving full instruction from him, occupy the pulpit. This training continues throughout the period of the meetings. In two instances a personal work committee sits in meeting daily about a table to compare notes, while the evangelistic campaign is on. Names are redistributed. The results of the quiet interviews with individuals are reported to the pastor, to whom the final effort is generally left in all cases.

PREPARATORY STEPS

During the weeks intervening before the meetings, not only are sermons and Sunday night services made distinctly evangelistic in character, but in the work of the Sunday school and other organizations stress is laid on the coming event. Where the group or district system [1] is in use, the leaders of each group work together to prepare the ground.

In several churches, opportunity is given at the close of each Sunday night service prior to the campaign for all who desire to unite with the church to declare themselves.

PUBLICITY

Shortly before the time for the meetings to begin, cards or folders announcing the dates, hours and subjects are generally distributed. The folder used by the church in Parma had on the outside:

> "For Everyone
> Time to Think."

After the announcement of the meetings was this statement:

> "Congregation in Charge."

This publicly proclaimed the fact, already mentioned, that responsibility for the meetings rests with the whole church. Upon the back of this leaflet was a serious address to the men headed:

> "What a Man Owes to the Church"

and ending:

> "Will You Do Your Part?"

[1] See Chapter VII, "Organizing the Church for the Program."

At the same time the meetings are in general widely advertised by posters, dodgers, and paid advertisements in the
local papers.[2]

Preceding any direct personal approach some churches
send personal letters to those whom they hope to win. This
is done especially in the case of prospective members who
once belonged to a church in another place but who, on
moving away, lost interest and severed connections. An
example of one such letter which was effectively used is
given:

My dear Mr. and Mrs. Mc——:
  In the past have you not had this thought, "Sometime I will
join the church here"?
  Sometimes have you not felt that it was your duty to do so
because the church needed you or because you've found yourself slipping from God and needed the church?
  Such thoughts are usually the promptings of God urging us
to do the right.
  The Communion of the Lord's Supper will be observed in the
church this Sunday morning. Those who love God and follow
Jesus will want to break bread together. Some are to join our
church then making confession of their Lord. Won't you join
with us? If you have church letters, bring them. If not, come
just the same. We want you; the letter can be obtained later
on.
  The hope of the world lies in a united Christendom. Your
strength is needed in the organization founded to establish the
Kingdom of God on earth. Your children will follow your
example.
  Your minister, in spite of an injury, will try to call. Think
the matter over, and make him happy by deciding to join the
Church of Christ in the community.
                              Your friend in Christ,[3]

———————   ———————

[2] Many of the methods described in the chapter on "Publicity"
have been used with success in evangelistic campaigns.
[3] In one instance, not among the cases used in this book, a survey
showed considerable groups of people untouched by the church's

THE EVANGELISTIC MEETINGS

Following a thorough preparation which may sometimes extend over an entire quarter of a year, the evangelistic services begin. The churches under study seldom employ a professional evangelist, although this has been done. Usually either the pastor or a brother minister from a neighboring community conducts the meeting. Much is made of music during the services. It is especially effective to select the hymns so that the thought they express shall run parallel to that of the sermon to be preached. Care in this matter is particularly important for congregational singing and for solos which some of these churches take pains to arrange for. Comparatively few, except those that take part in union meetings, use a large chorus choir.

The time of year most commonly chosen for this kind of a series of meetings is in the one or two weeks prior to Easter. Some churches prefer the week of prayer at the beginning of January, and still others hold meetings early in the fall. The time must be arranged with a view to the convenience of the community, the custom of the church, the pressure of farm work, which is greater in some seasons than in others. In some communities it is necessary to take into consideration even the phase of the moon. During the full moon, travel along country roads to evening services is far easier.

OTHER EVANGELISTIC METHODS

The Sunday school furnishes the readiest field for evangelistic endeavor. Most of those who join these churches come to them from their own Sunday schools. They are brought to the decision to join the church by three methods other than that of the evangelistic campaign. Every school

influence. The pastor gathered together the leaders of the various lodges and societies in the community and secured their help in planning a series of special church services designed to help the community. The organizations each allowed one person to represent them in a community conference. In this instance church attendance was quadrupled by following the plan, and sharp intensive work brought many of these people afterward into the church.

attempts definitely to enlist pupils of proper age in the church; and about a third of them observe Decision Day as a means toward this end. In almost all the schools there is more or less personal work by the teacher, usually under the advice and instruction of the pastor. Then there is the confirmation class conducted at certain seasons of each year for young people of the required age either within the Sunday school or at other than Sunday school hours. The members of this class preparing for church membership are, however, recruited for the most part from the Sunday school.

SPECIAL DAYS

Prior to certain special days, such as Easter and Rally Day, which are set aside in a number of the churches as church-joining days, prospective members are visited by the pastor and often by officers or workers from the church. The invitation is extended in this quiet, personal way, frequently over the table at the home of the prospective member. Many such visits are made, under assignment, by members of official boards or by volunteer parish visitors in churches that have this system.

CLASSES TO PREPARE FOR CHURCH MEMBERSHIP

The results of the Interchurch World Movement surveys showed that the 20 per cent. of churches which had classes to prepare prospects for church membership, or as the liturgical churches know them, confirmation classes, gained proportionately four times as many members as the churches that lacked such classes. More than half of these churches have such classes.

Perhaps the most thorough system of all is followed by the Mamrelund Lutheran Church at Stanton, Iowa,[4] where from a graded class within the Sunday school the pupils pass, at the age of fourteen or fifteen, to a confirmation class taught from January to September by a competent

[4] See the Committee's publication "Churches of Distinction in Town and Country" (George H. Doran Company), Chapter XI.

Sunday school teacher. This training is supplemented by instruction from the pastor for several hours every Saturday afternoon during eight months. Classes in the Bible, catechism, and Bible history are included in the curriculum and in addition there are lectures on themes relating to the Christian life. At the close of the course those young people who are willing to unite with the church have the rite of confirmation administered to them with a knowledge of all that it means. Besides this course for adolescents, the pastor gives lectures on Sunday afternoons to persons above the age of seventeen. Persons enter this class without pledging themselves to join the church. In the year preceding the survey, the class numbered twenty-five. At its final meeting the pastor said: "At the confirmation service next Sunday evening there will be in the front of the church twenty-five chairs waiting for you. I hope you are all ready to come out on the right side." On the appointed evening the church was so crowded that chairs were put in all the available spaces, even in the vestibules. Gradually the twenty-five members took the chairs placed ready for them. When the service began the twenty-five were all there.

FOLLOWING UP THE RESULTS

There is too general a tendency in churches holding protracted meetings to feel that when converts are once enrolled nothing more need be done; but this feeling is not in evidence in the churches studied. These churches have such thorough knowledge of their own fields and of their needs that new members are quickly assigned tasks in the church organizations. Consecration is in this way strengthened by service. First of all, the effort is made to align each new member with at least one church organization. Sunday school pupils are, of course, already aligned. With the thorough preparation which these churches make, most new converts already have contacts with some other members and organizations. Some churches schedule their mission study classes immediately after their greatest in-taking of members. Some conduct training groups for specific tasks.

NURTURING BOYS AND GIRLS

Some churches give further training to their boys and girls who have become members of the church. At Dayton, for example, for two years after their admission, the young members receive instruction from their Sunday school teachers in the Intermediate Catechism of their denomination. At the end of this period they are questioned upon their work during a Sunday evening service devoted to the purpose. The boys and the girls are pitted against each other and are closely questioned as to their studies. Older members are present, and the whole exercise is made interesting to all.

At Sacaton, Arizona, there are among the Indians nine catechetical classes graded as to age and enrolling a total of 177. All but one of these classes are taught by Indians. Once a year all members are asked if they have come to the place where they are willing to unite with the church.

CIRCUIT EVANGELISM

Holding evangelistic services on a circuit, particularly a large one, is a very difficult problem. The minister of the Methodist Circuit at Larned, Kansas, solved it in an unusual way by having each of his four churches hold services for one week with their own members in charge while the pastor was in command during the second week. The minister spent several weeks prior to these meetings in preparing his leaders for the enterprise, using methods that have been outlined above. It was no small venture of faith to trust a week of evangelistic services to each of four churches without any pastoral oversight. The plan seemed to work with accumulative interest. The net result showed a considerable increase in the membership of every church on the circuit.

INDIANS SET THE PACE

The Indians at Sacaton, Arizona, in addition to using a number of the methods which have been described, set an example to other Christians in that frequently, for months at a time, they are willing to leave their work to go to a village of pagan Indians and do evangelistic work among them. One convert, lately a hard drinker, was the only one to respond to a call for such work in a mining village where conditions were very bad. The minister let him go with strong misgivings. He made a striking success. He cleaned up politics, stopped some bad drinking places, and got a new sheriff as a result of his work. This man has since become one of the assistants in the Mission.

EXTENSION EVANGELISM

Virtually all of the churches located in villages and towns extend their influence considerably beyond the corporate limits of their communities. Three churches in particular have penetrated far into the areas of no-man's land such as are found too often outlying small communities. The California Federated Church at Imperial has a Gospel Extension Department which conducts Sunday schools and services at four or five nearby points with emphasis on evangelism. Volunteer lay workers handle all of this work under the direction of a minister. At Arnold, Nebraska, the Baptist Church discovered that the congregations in the town included few if any from the surrounding country. Investigation showed that whole neighborhoods had few or no church members. Therefore this congregation, by extending an energetic campaign that centered in the new church plant in the town, has carried its evangelistic work to the farming population. Three Sunday schools and preaching points have been established in neighborhoods where before there was no religious work.

The same plan is being used in two or three other churches, in one instance under the direction of an extension worker who is employed by the congregation. It is of course a plan that is particularly applicable in the larger parish type of work by which a church seeks to minister not only to those upon its roll but also to people of the entire area in which it is felt that its responsibility lies.[5]

[5] See "Churches of Distinction in Town and Country," Chapter VI.

One question the experience of these churches entirely fails to answer. It is impossible to tell from their records whether the church that conducts an evangelistic campaign is more successful in enlisting new members than the church that does not. The proportionate gain in the two groups of these churches is almost identical. There are some churches in which the normal type of evangelistic campaign simply would not work, and pastors for the most part have been wise enough not to try it. Here and there it has been attempted and has failed; not because it was a campaign but because the conditions required at that time a different kind of evangelism. There are other places where an evangelistic campaign has been attempted with success. Many people, especially Sunday school members accustomed to such meetings, wait till the meetings are held to declare themselves and unite with the church. This, of course, is a matter of tradition and inheritance rather than of method; and in the last analysis it is probably by such considerations that the success or failure of an evangelistic campaign is determined.

SUMMARY

The evangelistic program of any church may therefore, with good reason, include many of the following features:

1. An annual house-to-house religious census or survey, union in nature where there is more than one church, to locate the unchurched and ascertain the ideas of the people regarding the program of the church.
2. An enlistment of the entire membership in the evangelistic work through letters, cottage prayer meetings, training of personal workers, publicity, and the actual use of membership in services, especially in outlying neighborhoods.
3. The cultivation of all prospective members through every possible person or agency by means of—
    (a) A class to prepare for church membership.
    (b) Decision Day in the Sunday school.

(c) Use of social occasions for tactful cultivation of prospects.

(d) Use of special occasions as church-joining days.

(e) Evangelistic note in sermons prior to an evangelistic campaign, if one is held, and at intervals throughout the year.

(f) An evangelistic campaign.

(g) An effort to reach the entire community and every age, sex and economic group within it.

4. A careful follow-up of the campaign, and an enlistment of new members in the service and activities of the church.

BIBLIOGRAPHY

The Making of a Country Parish—HARLOW S. MILLS. Missionary Education Movement in the United States and Canada, 1914. 126 pp. $.50.

Parish Evangelism—F. L. FAGLEY. Revell, 1921. 121 pp. $1.00.

Evangelism—F. W. HANNAN. Abingdon Press. $1.50.

TOPICS FOR DISCUSSION

1. State how a church may best bring into membership persons of the following groups:

    (a) Children of members.

    (b) Children of non-church members.

    (c) Persons belonging to churches elsewhere.

    (d) Church-goers, outside the membership.

    (e) People in outlying districts who in the ordinary course of things come into contact with a church only at weddings and funerals.

2. Ask a dozen men who are outside the church why they are not church members, and classify their replies.

3. Why do people who have been active church workers for years often leave their church letters at the bottom of their trunks when they move to a new place? What special measures may be taken to win such people to membership in a church of their new community?

4. "The best tract is the tract in boots." Explain and discuss this statement.

5. State reasons why so many churches fail to retain a hold on their Sunday school children after the age of 14.

6. In holding Decision Day in the Sunday school, how may

those in charge guard against the danger of the same child making a "decision" year after year?

7. Give whatever suggestions you can in regard to classes to prepare for church membership. Should they be connected with the Sunday school? When and where should they be held? Over how long a period should the session last? What should be the subjects taught? Should the teacher be a Sunday school teacher, or the pastor?

8. How old ought children to be before they are permitted to join the church?

9. Which of the three times of year usually chosen for special services—the first week in January, the week or weeks before Easter, and some time in the fall—seems to you to have the most advantages? State those advantages.

10. Give reasons for beginning preparation some time in advance for a series of special meetings. How long should this preparatory period last?

11. Why do successful churches do well in conducting their evangelistic campaigns as churches, rather than in leaving the matter entirely in the hands of the pastor or of a paid evangelist?

12. Compare the effectiveness as leaders of evangelistic services of the pastor, a neighboring pastor, a professional evangelist.

13. What danger lies in the practice of some churches of receiving immediately into full membership persons professing a change of heart under excitement of a revival service?

14. Suggest a course of action by which persons converted at special services may be brought into permanent and mutually helpful relationship with the church.

15. In your own community, are evangelistic meetings held with good effect? Explain.

Chapter II

WORSHIP AND SERVICES

Worship has been from time immemorial one of the most important expressions of religion. Whether the devotional spirit of the services might have been weakened by the multiplicity of activities in the churches studied, was a pressing question in the minds of the investigators. But the testimony of the field workers on this point was almost unanimous—the services of worship were found to fulfill their purpose. These churches surpass the average church in this part of their program as much as in their other activities.

Reports from the field frequently alluded to the "atmosphere" of services. This atmosphere is partly explained, perhaps, by the feeling of expectancy with which the people week after week enter the sanctuary. They come desiring to worship. In the past they have not been disappointed. Another partial explanation concerns the ministers. These men are described as quiet but dynamic, restrained but forceful; and such a temper helps to arouse a spirit of worship.

Study of the mechanics of the services shows that these churches pay close attention to every detail. In the churches of liturgical denominations the liturgy was read not as a mere matter of form but with understanding and feeling. Of one pastor of a non-liturgical church a member exclaimed: "His prayers alone are worth his salary." The scripture readings, too, are selected with care and read with understanding and impressiveness. The ministers do not look upon the prayers and the reading of scripture as mere preliminaries to the sermon. Every detail is directed toward an end; and that end is to lift the people out of their ordinary material concerns into the realm of the Spirit.

MUSIC

The music of these churches is such as to add to the impressiveness of the worship. Many of the churches have pipe organs, and not infrequently the organ has recently been installed. The music is usually under the charge of trained musicians, some of them volunteers, others working on salary. Some of these leaders have for years given considerable time to weekly rehearsals, to preparation for special musical features like trios or quartettes, and to the long periods of training necessary for rendering oratorios or cantatas. One church, besides having a mixed choir, has a double male quartette; another has both junior and senior choirs; another has a chorus; others have bands or orchestras.

SERMONS

The sermons showed a considerable variety. The ministers do not over-emphasize any one phase of Christian experience. They are equally at home in dealing with the ethical aspects of Christianity and with its greater spiritual realities. They do not shrink from a vigorous application of the principles of Jesus Christ either to a local situation or to the great mysteries of life. As one of these men said: "The first element of success in the ministry of a small town community church is emphasis on those things that all have in common. The minister must not ride theological hobbies. As sure as he does, the people disagree with him. I don't preach special beliefs. I do preach the Kingdom of God as hard as I can."

THE MORNING SERVICE

A number of these churches make a contrast between their morning and evening services. In the morning comes the formal service of worship, when the theme of the sermon is related to some great fundamental Christian truth, and when the music is dignified and classical.

Worship for Children

The opening part of the morning service is frequently devoted to the children. From Sunday school they march into the church for their own brief period of worship and a sermonette, sometimes illustrated. At Collbran, though adults may attend, none may enter after the opening of the service. At the conclusion of their special exercises the children leave. At the Methodist Church of Rolla, Missouri, the children are regularly organized as a junior congregation. Once a month they have a special morning service, with their own choir and ushers.

THE SUNDAY EVENING SERVICE

The service in the evening is less formal. There is more congregational singing, and this may be led by such groups as a junior choir or a Sunday school orchestra. At the Lutheran Church of Stanton, Iowa, every other Sunday evening service is preceded by an organ recital of classical music; and the singing is led by a vested choir of fifty members who also frequently render special numbers. Some churches occasionally devote the whole evening hour to a service of song. Such musical services are not designed to make it unnecessary for the minister to preach a sermon; they form parts of a plan covering the whole church year, and are always organized around some one idea.

The Sermon

The evening sermon deals with some topic of ethical and often of local interest. The Baptist Church of New Monmouth, New Jersey, generally plans to cover at the evening services the wider interests of the church. The first Sunday evening of each month is given to the church and missions; and frequent use is made of the stereopticon. The second Sunday evening concerns the church and the school. The third is devoted to the church and the government; to such subjects as "Law Enforcement," "The Duties of Christian Citizenship," and "The Ethics of Taxation." On the fourth and fifth Sundays the theme is the community; and among more usual topics a place is given to "The Home" and to "Good Health."

Moving-Pictures

Moving-pictures are used in the evening by a number of churches either to illustrate Biblical scenes and passages or to present ethical truths. One Sunday evening program at a frontier church included not only the picture but a violin solo, congregational singing of favorite hymns, scripture readings to illustrate the picture which was Biblical, and a brief talk by the pastor.

Addresses by Invited Speakers

Occasionally the address at an evening service is made by an outsider. The use of special speakers may, of course, be a confession of laziness on the part of the pastor. The wise minister, however, is eager to induce men better qualified than he to speak on topics of special interest and appeal. Among the speakers who had recently addressed the churches studied were a judge of a State Supreme Court, a Y. M. C. A. secretary, denominational leaders, and returned missionaries.

Using the Membership

To give variety to the evening program, some churches put the service in charge of one or another of the organizations, such as the men's class or the young people's society. Sometimes an individual leads the service; sometimes the group in charge presents a program.

Forum

None of the churches makes use of the open forum on Sunday evenings. This recent development has proved valuable, however, in the experience of certain churches investigated by the Committee on Social and Religious Surveys in other rural studies. At Sheridan, Wyoming, for example, a forum is conducted under the auspices of the men's clubs of two churches which draws an average attendance of four hundred. Its principles are as follows:

The complete development of democracy in America.

A common meeting ground for all the people in the interest of truth and mutual understanding, and for the cultivation of community spirit.

The freest and fullest open discussion of all vital questions affecting human welfare.

Participation on the part of the audience from the Forum Floor whether by questions or discussion.

The freedom of the Forum management from responsibility for utterances by speakers from the platform or floor.

Among the subjects presented have been Community Problems, The Church and Industrial Conflict, The Golden Rule in Business: Is It Practicable?, The Farmers' Movement in America, Bolshevism, Feeding the World: Is It America's Job?[1]

In another instance a forum held by a country church doubled the evening attendance in three months. A subject is given out in advance and a committee of six is appointed, three representing one side and three the other. The formal debate is followed by a general discussion. Over half the audience is made up of young people.

THE MID-WEEK SERVICE

A number of these churches have strong mid-week meetings which are not stereotyped but vary from week to week, usually in accordance with a previously arranged program. At Rolla, Missouri, the congregation is divided into groups, one of which in the absence of the minister takes charge of the meeting and leads a discussion upon modern implications of some part of the New Testament. An interesting experiment has been made in Garrettsville, Ohio, where the United Church has set apart the evening hours of every Wednesday as "Church Night." At six o'clock the women

[1] See the Committee's publication, "The Church on the Changing Frontier" (George H. Doran Company), page 87.

serve a supper at cost to all that may come; and the supper is followed by community singing lasting about twenty minutes. Then there is a short devotional service; and after that either an open forum or an address, perhaps by some outside speaker, followed by discussion. The average attendance is just short of 100. Church nights are also observed by the Presbyterian Church of Davis, California, a short address being delivered on some topic of community interest adapted to attract young people.

At the Brick Presbyterian Church at Perry, New York, every other Wednesday evening is devoted to a course in Church History. The class uses a textbook, copies of which are owned by twenty-four families; and the average attendance is thirty-five. The mid-week service of Grace Church, at Spencer, Iowa, is varied in character, sometimes taking the form of a study course in evangelism; sometimes that of an old-fashioned Methodist experience meeting; while at other times there are talks by the minister. The Presbyterian Church in Novato, California, has replaced the prayer-meeting with a moving-picture program.

One of the most unusual contributions to worship made by any of these churches is found at Buckhorn, Kentucky. At irregular hours once a day for years, a woman of this congregation has rung the church bell. That ringing has become known as the "Prayer Bell." Whenever it is heard through the mountain valleys, every one stops for a moment of prayer. If the children are on the playground, instantly there is silence and reverence. If transactions are going on at the community store, proprietor and purchaser, at the sound of the bell, stand for a moment together before their God.

On the program of these churches the services of worship hold a conspicuous place. The churches do not attract their members solely through their Sunday schools and their community activities. They make their appeals through many-sided programs of Christian service, which include religious education, community service, and worship. Among these indispensable activities, each church apportions time and effort in its own way.

SUMMARY

Every detail of the service is considered important, and each is made to contribute to the effect of the whole.

Music is used in many forms and ways.

Sermons are varied in topic but cover in the course of a year the full range of Christian experience. For the children some of the churches provide a service of worship of their own.

The moving-picture or stereopticon is used at evening services to illustrate Biblical events and moral truths. Use may also be made of a forum. Some of the churches conduct mid-week services along familiar lines; but a larger number are trying new departures.

BIBLIOGRAPHY

Public Worship—T. HARWOOD PATTISON. American Baptist Publication Society. 1900. 265 pp. $1.25.

Art of Public Worship—PERCY DEARMER. London: Standard Publishing Company. 1920. 213 pp. $2.00.

The prayers that close the daily reading in Dr. Harry Emerson Fosdick's books, "The Meaning of Prayer" ($1.15), "The Meaning of Service" ($1.25), and "The Meaning of Faith" ($1.35) (all published by the Association Press), should prove very suggestive. In this connection should also be mentioned "Prayers of the Social Awakening" by Walter Rauschenbusch (published by Pilgrim Press—$1.00).

TOPICS FOR DISCUSSION

1. "Worship exists primarily for the sake of making articulate the voice of the Spirit. And for this a group of earnest souls is a prime requisite." [2] If this statement of the purpose of worship does not satisfy you, write a substitute. Then, having in mind the purpose of worship, draw practical conclusions as to the morning service of the country church, considering in particular:

   (1) Frequency
   (2) Attendance
   (3) Music
   (4) Sermon
   (5) Other parts of the program.

[2] From an editorial in the "Community Churchman," January, 1923 p. 260.

2. "Will the radio supplant the church?"[3] Support your opinion.

3. Is the recital of the Apostles' Creed a helpful part of worship for an audience today? Explain.

4. Several collections of prayers for common worship have been recently published. May judicious use of such prayers, and of the Episcopal prayer book, contribute to the effectiveness of the service for churches whose worship is free? If so, how?

5. What connection is possible between the spirit of worship and church music? How adequately does the music of your church fulfill its office? How may it be improved?

6. Explain the psychological reason why many people believe that the church auditorium should be kept sacred to worship. Where there is no other place for entertainments and social occasions, what should be done?

7. "The day is past when one man can stand up and tell everybody what's what." Discuss this assertion, made by a thoughtful woman living in the country. Mention any tendencies that may have lessened the authority of the preacher. How should the new attitude of his hearers be met by the minister?

8. "I see a Sunday morning in the future, with all the people gathered in one great temple for devotion. . . . Houses are empty, theaters closed, books and newspapers laid aside, the noise of the streets become a silence. The Community is at worship!"[4] Discuss the practicability of:
   (1) Getting everybody to church.
   (2) Getting all sorts of people into the same church.

9. State the respective advantages, for the training of children in worship, of the three following courses:
   (1) A separate service.
   (2) A part of the general service, including a brief children's sermon.
   (3) The modification of the whole service in consideration of the needs of children.

10. What religious needs of your community, not fully met by the Sunday morning service, should be satisfied on Sunday evening? Outline a series of services lasting from the first of November to the end of April, adapted to meet these needs.

11. "In too many communities . . . religion is treated no longer

[3] Title of an editorial in a religious periodical.
[4] J. H. Holmes, "New Churches for Old," p. 312, Dodd, 1922.

as a primary need, but is introduced surreptitiously between stereopticon slides." [5] Does this statement set forth a real danger? If so, how may the danger be avoided?

12. If the prayer meeting is attended only by half a dozen aged saints, what should the church do—drop it altogether, modify it, or substitute something else? Make your answer specific and contributory.

[5] Shailer Mathews, "Scientific Management in the Churches," p. 2.

Chapter III

RELIGIOUS EDUCATION

Religious education in these churches gives evidence of hopeful experimentation in better methods of training their constituency.

The chapter on "The Plant and Its Equipment" tells of the efforts made to provide their church schools with the best equipment within their means. Almost all now have separate rooms or curtained spaces for certain classes. The reader will find information regarding these and other parts of the equipment in the chapter referred to.

The total Sunday school enrollment of these churches equals about 90 per cent. of the total resident church membership. In twenty of the churches the enrollment of the Sunday school is larger than that of the church. In six the school is decidedly the smaller; but there is an unusually large school in connection with an even larger church in each of four of these. The high ratio is even more significant in the light of the fact that half the pupils come from farm homes, and of the further fact that the parishes are far more extended than is the average parish.

Non-Evangelical Pupils

In about a fourth of the communities in which these churches are situated, there are non-evangelical elements in the population which are either not reached or not closely held by religious institutions of their own. From families among these a small number of pupils, most of them Roman Catholic, attend the Sunday schools. At Bingham Canyon, Utah, the regular attendants of the Sunday school include thirteen children of Mormon families. These few schools draw more pupils from non-evangelical groups than do all the 1,000 schools investigated by the Committee on Social and Religious Surveys in its follow-up study of the Town and Country surveys begun by the Interchurch World Movement.

Attendance

The average attendance, for all the schools taken together, is 66 per cent. of the total enrollment; which is virtually the same as the average for the schools in the twenty-five typical counties surveyed by the Committee on Social and Religious Surveys. As for the schools under the average, almost all were contending with serious difficulties, such as Sunday work that kept people away, unusually large parishes, very bad roads in the spring, or student members absent during long vacations. Ten of the schools had a proportion of attendance about equal to the average; the other twelve exceeded it, six reaching 75 per cent. or more, with three of these exceeding 88 per cent. The records of these last schools approximate or exceed the ordinary ratio of attendance of public schools. On the whole, then, the record of attendance for the schools of these forty churches is decidedly good.

For this there are several reasons. (1) Their work is of interest and value. In the younger classes, for example, handwork and sand-tables are commonly used in teaching the lesson. (2) The school spirit is high. (3) Many of the teachers make personal calls at the homes of their pupils. (4) A large part of the general program of the church is, in many cases, conducted through organized classes. Eligibility for athletic teams depends upon regular attendance at Sunday school. (5) The schools themselves emphasize regularity of attendance by using perfect-attendance diplomas, by drawing attention to the record of the day in comparison with that of the corresponding Sunday of the previous year, and by rewarding perfect attendance throughout a given period with honorable mention or prizes. (6) A healthy rivalry is cultivated between classes and between departments of the school.

The organization of these church schools follows the usual lines. The differences between them and many other schools is that in every one of them the organization works. The superintendent is usually a man prominent in the community. A few of the larger schools have two superintendents; and in the very largest schools, which are graded, a superintendent has been chosen for each department. The organization, which follows the usual lines, includes in the school proper the departments suggested by the International Sunday School Association, namely, Beginners, Primary, Junior, Intermediate, Senior and Adult. In addition, there is a Cradle Roll and a Home Department, both of which are recruiting grounds for the school itself.

To the practice suggested in the abundant literature upon these departments, no significant exceptions were discovered.

Home Department and Cradle Roll

The Home Department is adapted ideally for those unable to attend the church school. Many such, especially shut-ins, are found in the Home Departments of the schools under consideration. Those not so incapacitated as to make their attendance impossible, are urged by several schools to join adult classes. The Cradle Roll, too, is carefully watched. Birthdays of the children are not forgotten. Several schools hold annual parties for the babies and their mothers. One church has appropriated to the Cradle Roll an attractive room in the church building, which has been decorated with flowers and with pictures of the members. Here there is held for the babies a service with a brief and simple program.

The parish visitors coöperate with the Cradle Roll Superintendent. The church shows genuine interest in the development of the children.[1]

Classes

The number of classes varies from three or four in the very smallest schools, to thirty in the largest. In all these classes the morale is high. Many are organized and have names and mottoes.[2] Since the work of the school is taken in real earnest, there is no difficulty in enlisting the interest of the classes in the curriculum.

CURRICULUM

Graded Lessons

More than half the schools use graded lessons. For the most part, these are the International Graded, but several employ other systems, a few of which are rather ambitious in scope. Graded lessons, of course, call for some home work. The schools report no difficulty in having this work done. The class and school spirit, the interest in the work itself, the excellence of the teaching, all help to insure success. Graded lessons are found even in some of the smaller schools, under the modified graded plan which provides for each department, one class covering the work of the department in several successive years. The experience of these churches shows that the use of graded lessons is possible in the church schools in the country and in the smaller towns.

Bible Study for Public School Credit

Three of the communities recognize the importance of Bible study by giving it public school credit. The work is

[1] One church not included in this investigation distributed the government bulletins on child-care to the mothers of the babies on the Cradle Roll. Another church holds in its building a child-clinic where, under the wise guidance of a woman physician, it is but a short step from discussion of the child's physical to that of his spiritual welfare.

[2] See chapter on "Work for Age and Sex Groups."

done either in connection with the public school, in classes taught by the minister, or in classes of the church school. The first method is used in Bible study in the high school at Dayton, Indiana, where a part of the regular work of the Junior year is a course on the life of Christ. Bible study by special classes of the church school is given credit in the public schools of Whiting, Iowa, and in those of Montrose, Colorado. At the end of the year there is an examination; and the pupils who pass it receive credit for a half-year's work.

At Duncannon, Pennsylvania, a similar plan is now being developed. Daily religious instruction, in connection with that given in the Sunday schools, will be provided in the public schools if all the churches agree to the plan, and if the teachers employed for the classes are of as high grade as the present public school teachers.

CHURCH SCHOOL TEACHERS AND THEIR PREPARATION

More than a sweet Christian character is demanded of the teachers in the schools of the successful churches. An honest effort is made to select individuals fitted to the particular task.

One-fourth of the teachers are men, a surprisingly high average. Another cause of surprise is the number of teachers belonging to the professional class. Among these the doctors lead, a fact that is a tribute to the program and to the ideals of these schools; for no one is busier than a country doctor. His investment of time in such an enterprise is a real contribution.

Training Classes

Half these churches give their teachers definite training. In some instances the class meets each week; sometimes the sessions are less frequent. The meeting is held either during the hour of the church school or on the evening of the mid-week service. The various courses used have been recommended either by the denominational authorities in religious education or by the state or national Sunday school association. A number of the courses cover three or four years, and include not only the Bible but the elements of pedagogy and child psychology. A number of the churches supplement the work of the teacher of the training class by bringing in on occasion specialists in different phases of religious education, whose lectures are followed by general discussion. These teacher-training courses enroll both prospective teachers and teachers in service.

Workers' Conferences

In addition to training classes, many of the churches conduct workers' conferences or boards of religious education. Such gatherings are often called faculty meetings. The business routine of the school, which too often consumes the time of a teacher's meeting, is sometimes relegated to a small Executive Committee, so that the whole period may be given over to the discussion of improved methods. The Methodist school at Prairie Grove, Arkansas, requires from every teacher a monthly report under sixteen heads. Upon the blank provided the teacher must state how he has increased the knowledge and interest of the class; to what extent he has followed up absentees; and how much time he has devoted to preparation of the lessons and to other Sunday school activities. Space is also provided for suggestions from the teacher.

EXTRA-CURRICULUM ACTIVITIES

The church schools under consideration utilize for their purposes a number of special occasions. At Christmas and Easter are special services for the whole school intended to fix in the minds of the children the meaning of these festivals. In such celebrations a large place is given to music and pageantry.

Rally Day

On Rally Day, these schools make special efforts to rally the members for the work of the opening year and to enlist additional members. Some of the schools have two Rally Days, one in the fall at the end of harvest and another in the spring after the roads have dried up so that attendance at church is more regular. For these Rally Days, the schools make careful preparation. They stimulate attendance in the ways described in the chapter on "Publicity." The teachers visit the homes of their pupils. Every detail, from program to decorations, is referred to some member of the faculty or workers' council. Preparation for the fall rally frequently begins in early August. Just before Rally Day some schools conduct a religious census or survey. Some churches have adopted names suggestive of the activities of their respective regions. At Collbran, Colorado, for example, Rally Day has been rechristened "Round-up Day." A few schools have set aside the entire week prior to the Rally Day as church school week. Meetings every evening cover the different departments and activities; and during the week a special drive for new members is conducted.

Decision Day

To Decision Day reference has already been made in the chapter on "Evangelism." Where this is used, it is not a mere matter of form. In some schools the decision of a child for the Christian life results in his enrollment in a class to prepare for church membership.

Other Days

Almost all the schools observe Promotion Day, on which pupils who have finished the work of one grade or department are transferred to a higher grade or another department. Other schools make use of a Stewardship Day, on which the principle of stewardship is impressed by appropriate lessons, responsive readings and hymns. Still others, on such occasions as Thanksgiving and Christmas, take offerings for special benevolent enterprises.

General Social Occasions

Most of the churches, in addition to the activities of organized classes, have various social occasions for the school as a whole. Chief among these is the annual picnic. In a few communities this is an interdenominational affair and in others a community affair. The arrangements are usually planned so as to provide enjoyment for the whole family, the various activities enlisting every age- and sex-group, so that the day becomes a veritable play festival. Preparations are made with extreme care, and the program is carried out with dispatch. Of other socials for the school as a whole, some are held quarterly, some on particular occasions such as Hallowe'en, Valentine's Day, or St. Patrick's Day.

INTERDENOMINATIONAL COÖPERATION

More than half the schools are active in the larger work of religious education, being represented by delegates at institutes or state and county conventions. These delegates for the most part pay their own expenses; but in case of larger meetings farther away the school often assumes financial responsibility. The benefit of representation in such meetings is fully recognized by these schools. To the application of ideas received at such a convention one of them attributes the fact that in the past few years it has nearly trebled its attendance.

DAILY VACATION BIBLE SCHOOL

For over a decade progressive city churches have conducted Daily Vacation Bible Schools. The experiences of certain of the churches surveyed proves that this form of work is also useful in town and country. Such schools were conducted by eleven churches of the forty, a very high proportion. Among the eleven were churches in towns, in villages and in open country. Activities of the various schools vary somewhat. They include religious instruction, mission study, Bible study, dramatization of Biblical incidents, organized play, story-telling hours, and classes in carpentry, basketry, sewing and home-making. Liturgical churches also taught the catechism. Several schools used sand-tables, especially for the younger classes. During the course of the morning, every school devoted a period to organized play.

Leadership

The securing of teachers for this work presents difficulties that are serious but not insuperable. Responsibility was assumed, in several instances, by the minister or his wife; in other cases by teachers, by college students home for vacation, or by married women with training and leisure. In a few instances the leaders gave their services; but these were cases in which the schools lasted only two weeks. In all other cases, full-time teachers were paid. The money needed was raised, in part by an offering from the children enrolled, and in part by one from parents who attended the final demonstration session of the school. The full-time workers, of whom there were from three to six, were assisted by volunteers, who in one case numbered seventeen. To house the enterprise, public school buildings were turned over to the church in two instances. In one of these the school was an interdenominational affair whose creation was inspired, and which was led, by the church covered in this study.

Terms and Enrollment

The average term was one month. A few of the schools ran six weeks; some of the others only two. In none was the enrollment under fifty; in six it exceeded 100. The proportion of attendance fell below 75 per cent. in only one instance. In other words, the Daily Vacation Bible School made a better attendance record during its session than the Sunday schools of these churches made during the year.

Parents were usually much impressed by the work of the school, and almost all the churches were encouraged by enthusiastic comments. One business man became so much interested that he asked permission to have a moving-picture reel made of the activities. Later this was shown at the State Synod of the denomination concerned. So far as known, it is the only reel of its kind in the country.

MISSIONARY EDUCATION

In each of these church schools the curriculum includes mission study. The lessons are sometimes weekly and sometimes monthly. In a few instances, a longer period is set aside once a quarter. In giving instruction regarding missionary matters the schools use either of two methods, or both. They specialize in the study of the particular field which is served by a missionary or native worker supported by the school or by the foreign pastor of the church and use for the purpose letters sent from the field; or they use leaflets or textbooks, denominational or not, and conduct the recitations by questions and answers. The church in the Baptist Rural Parish of Arnold, Nebraska, has even set aside in the tower of its new building a Missionary Room. Here are to be gathered curios from the foreign field and pictures of missionary work. In this room the classes of the school will meet in rotation under the direction of a special teacher of Missions.

Mission Study Outside the Church School

Other church organizations study Missions, either topically or through the use of denominational or interdenominational textbooks. The activity in this field of societies of women and of young women is well known. Young people's societies or junior societies often include in their program for the year provision for mission study either at regular intervals or weekly during certain periods. A few Sunday school classes devote to the subject periods outside the regular session. Groups of small children, such as the King's Heralds of some Methodist churches, follow with surprising regularity the little mission courses prepared for them. Of such groups several of our churches have from two to five, with a combined roll for each church of over a hundred children. In connection with the Methodist Episcopal church at Rolla, Missouri, for instance, 116 children in five groups hold monthly meetings two and a half hours long, at which the combined average attendance is 107.

Schools of Missions

In four churches missionary interest is so keen that the entire congregation in each case is annually organized into a graded school of missions. The Interdenominational Text Books for different age-groups are used. These schools meet once a week for six weeks, sometimes on Sunday evenings at the hour usually devoted to Christian Endeavor; in other cases on the evening of a week-day. At Imperial, California, the session is held Sunday evening, from six o'clock to seven; then refreshments are served and afterward the entire school attends the evening service. To make their teaching the more interesting and impressive, all these schools of missions use stereopticon slides and pageantry. The Middle Octoraro Presbyterian church, situated in the open country, divides its school membership into seven groups, making it convenient for sessions to be held at the seven neighborhood centers of the parish. Each group has two teachers enlisted from the residents of the neighborhood. Last year, the average attendance for each group was twenty-two per week, so that the total weekly average was 154, equivalent to more than half the resident church membership. The teachers have, of course, the advice and assistance of the pastor; but as he was the leader of one of the sections, he could not visit any of the others. This interesting variation of method shows how a church with a large parish can follow its members into their home neighborhoods.

Other Methods of Missionary Education

The churches that either support or assist in supporting workers on the foreign field, utilize in missionary education

letters from these foreign representatives. Frequent reference has been made to the place given to pageantry. Some
of these pageants proved so popular that they were repeated
before audiences averaging more than 200. The churches
also circulate denominational periodicals, both general and
missionary; distribute leaflets; and utilize to the full the
resources and the property of the Boards of Home and
Foreign Missions. They also give missionary entertainments
and plays, provide stereopticon lectures, and invite special
speakers on missions.

LIFE SERVICE RECRUITS

During the past ten years eighteen of these forty churches
have sent sixty-four young people into professional Christian service. Of the sixty-four, forty-two have gone from
fourteen churches in the past five years.[3] Some of these
churches, and others which have no such representatives yet,
have several preparing for Christian service. One church
has eight of these recruits. In most of the churches there
are from one to three. This record, compared with that of
the average church, is phenomenal. The Committee on
Social and Religious Surveys has discovered that for the
entire country it has taken nearly three schools to furnish a
single recruit in the whole period of the last decade.

ENLISTING FOR PARISH SERVICE

Enlistment in local work also is important, and in the last
analysis a problem of education. This is not left to occasional appeals and haphazard volunteering on the part of the
membership in the various church activities. The strength
of these churches is derived in part from the constant pres-

[3] These figures do not include those from a nineteenth church,
Buckhorn, Kentucky. This church in the southern mountains has
a school as part of its plant. It has not kept complete records
but it is a conservative estimate that in the last decade more than
100 of its members have gone into one or another type of Christian
service. It is perhaps significant that the one church of all the
forty which controls the education of its community is the one
which has been able to accomplish this significant achievement.

sure put upon every available individual to give some regular service in connection with the church program. Several methods of enlistment are used. The Methodist Episcopal church of Duncannon, Pennsylvania, conducts a campaign for service at the time of the annual financial campaign. Members are asked to sign a church loyalty covenant which indicates the kind of service they are willing to accept. A similar method is used by quite a number of other churches, though "Volunteer Day," as it is sometimes called, is not set at the same time as the financial campaign. One of the cards distributed for volunteers to sign follows:

METHODIST EPISCOPAL CHURCH SOUTH
PRAIRIE GROVE, ARKANSAS
The Church with a Community Program
VOLUNTEER DAY

Realizing that the success of the church depends upon my efforts, I volunteer for the period of one year, to give my best to the MASTER in every way. And, to do special work as indicated:

1. Personal work...., 2. Sunday school work...., 3. Group work with boys...., 4. Group work with girls...., 5. Community Social Work...., 6. Gospel Team Work...., 7. Automobile Service...., 8. Epworth League Work...., 9. Prayer Meeting Work...., 10. Boosters' Work...., 11. Woman's Missionary Society Work...., 12. Junior Missionary Work...., 13. Choir Work...., 14. Gospel Visitation Work...., 15. General Church Work...., 16. Special Daily Prayer for Revival....

Many of us can do several different things; check with pencil the special works you will undertake for the coming year. "Give God Your Best."

.....................Name - - - Date ....

LEADERSHIP TRAINING

Constant efforts are made to train new leaders. Those who accept responsibility are made to exercise it. Membership on committees, wise distribution of chairmanships, duties in connection with social organizations and the social program are all helpful in developing in young, new, or diffident members those qualities of self-possession and leadership upon which so much of the program of these churches depends. Several of the churches have definite classes in leadership-training conducted for periods of from two to four months. In these classes matters of church leadership, social service, Bible Study, and missions are considered.[4]

SUMMARY

In regard to religious education, which is one of the most important tasks of the Church, these significant points stand out in the experience of the churches studied:

So far as possible, classes meet in separate rooms.

Attendance, which should equal at least 75 per cent. of the enrollment, is stimulated by good teaching, by personal calls in the follow-up of absentees, by rivalry between classes and by an adequate program.

The general types of organization follow the satisfactory systems recommended by denominational boards and by the International Sunday School Association. Many classes are organized.

The Home Department and the Cradle Roll are actively used for recruiting members for the school proper.

Graded lessons are in general use.

In connection with a few schools, Bible Study is conducted for high school credit.

The teachers are of high grade; and the schools use training-classes, workers' conferences and other means to assist the present teachers and to prepare new ones.

Special days celebrated include Christmas, Easter, Thanksgiving and Rally Day.

Social life is not neglected.

Denominational coöperation is general, and has proved valuable.

Several schools conduct successful Daily Vacation Bible Schools.

Mission study is part of the program of all the schools and of various other church organizations. A few churches have conducted successful Schools of Missions.

These churches have sent forth three times as many profes-

---

[4] One church not included within the forty has a junior member on each of the official boards and all important committees have at least one member under twenty-one years of age.

sional Christian workers proportionately in the past decade as have the churches of typical counties studied by the Committee on Social and Religious Surveys.

BIBLIOGRAPHY

The Sunday School at Work in Town and Country—WILLIAM H. BRABHAM. Doran, 1922. 217 pp. $1.50.

Week Day Religious Education—HENRY F. COPE. Doran, 1921. 191 pp. $1.50.

Organizing the Church School—HENRY F. COPE. Doran, 1922. $1.75. A Manual.

The Teens and the Rural Sunday School—JOHN L. ALEXANDER. Association Press, 1914. 151 pp. $.50.

Principles of Religious Teaching—W. C. BARCLAY. Abingdon Press. $1.00.

Many pamphlets of denominational boards and state Sunday school associations, covering all phases of the work of a church school.

Indiana Survey of Religious Education—WALTER S. ATHEARN. Committee on Social and Religious Surveys. 3 vols. (Forthcoming.)

MISSION STUDY:

Training World Christians: A Handbook in Missionary Education—GILBERT LOVELAND. Methodist Book Concern, 1921. 240 pp. $1.25.

How To Teach Training World Christians—GILBERT LOVELAND. Paper, $.20.

The King's Business: A Study of Increased Efficiency for Women's Missionary Societies—MAUD F. RAYMOND. Central Committee on the United Study of Foreign Missions. 1913.

Pamphlets of denominational boards, Foreign Missions Conference of North America and Missionary Education Movement.

TOPICS FOR DISCUSSION

1. "Sunday school," "church school," "Bible school," "school of religion"—What aspect is emphasized by each name? Which aspect is the most important? State clearly your personal conception of the aim of the Sunday school. How nearly is this ideal reached by your own school?

2. "One of the chief problems before the Sunday school today is how to make of it a real school." [1] What lessons may the Sunday school learn from the practice of the public school?

3. Get from the secretary of your school the average attendance and the enrollment (omitting Cradle Roll and Home Department) for the past year. What proportion of the enrollment was the average attendance? The per cent. of attendance for the public school in most places will average 85 per cent. and is sometimes over 95 per cent. How does the ratio for your Sunday school bear comparison with this public school standard? With the public school record in your own community?

4. Is a good Christian necessarily a good Sunday school teacher? State the principal qualification for a successful teacher of (1) children of kindergarten age, (2) boys of twelve, (3) girls of fourteen, (4) young men 18–25.

5. What may the Sunday school teacher learn by visiting the public school classes in which her pupils are enrolled?

6. The pastor of one of the forty churches believes that all boys should be taught by men. Do you agree with him? Give reasons for or against this opinion.

7. Of the boys and young men between 14 and 21 in your community, what proportion are enrolled in the Sunday school? Why are the others outside?

8. What can the men in the church do to keep the boys in Sunday school?

9. "In our Sunday school we young people have been made either the 'cracker' on the end of the adult whip, or the overhead to the 'kids.' We do not like either place." [2] How may a Sunday school prevent its young people feeling that they are in either of these uncomfortable positions?

10. "But what do we find in the Sunday schools? Study of Israelites, Canaanites, Midianites, Edomites, of no more importance to our age than Scythians and Bactrians." [3] Show how the study of the Bible may be made of great "importance to our age." What element of truth has Dr. Holmes's charge, as applied to some Sunday schools? Does it hit yours?

[1] Coe, George A., "Education in Religion and Morals," p. 287.
[2] Thompson, James V., "Handbook for Workers with Young People."
[3] Holmes, J. H., "New Churches for Old," p. 21.

11. Should the Bible be the only textbook in the Sunday school? If not, what subjects should also be treated?

12. "The educational efforts of the church . . . do not have Christian efficiency as their goal. The Sunday school is committed to informational ideals."[5] In what respects do the Sunday schools of our forty churches really pursue the ideal of Christian efficiency as distinct from the mere imparting of information? What is the state of things in this respect in your own Sunday school?

13. "Spiritual illiteracy abounds in the churches themselves."[6] Just what does Professor Coe mean by this? Do you consider the statement true? If so, how can the Sunday school help to remedy the condition?

14. "A church must ultimately rise and fall with its Sunday school. . . . And yet, I fancy, most churches will appropriate more money for a quartette choir than for maps, apparatus, textbooks, instruction, and other indispensable requirements of a thoroughly equipped Sunday school."[7] Make a list of items of equipment urgently needed by your own Sunday school, and ascertain the price of each. How does the total compare with the sum spent annually on the choir?

15. How may contests be so used that they may not be mere devices for "speeding up" but may have results that are deeper and more permanent?

16. If a church should include in the budget an appropriation for the support of the Sunday school, what would be the effect on
   (1) The attitude of the church to the Sunday school?
   (2) The attitude of the Sunday school to the church?

17. What lessons should children learn through the collection? How may these lessons be more deeply impressed through
   (1) Choice of the object to which money is applied?
   (2) Means by which this object is determined?
   (3) Lessons in stewardship from teachers and superintendent?
   (4) Christmas and Easter offerings?

[5] Mathews, Shailer, "Scientific Management in the Churches," p. 39.
[6] "Religious Breakdown of the Ministry." Journal of Religion, January, 1921. Vol. I, p. 18.
[7] Mathews, Shailer, ibid., p. 55.

18. What advantages has an organized Sunday school class as compared with other church societies for the same age-group?

19. What may a Sunday school do to prepare for its own perpetuation and progress through
    - (1) Cradle Roll?
    - (2) Teacher Training?
    - (3) Teachers' and officers' council?
    - (4) Sending delegates to conventions and conferences?

20. Describe specific methods by which the Sunday school may train up the men and women of the future to
    - (1) Attend church services.
    - (2) Contribute to church finances.
    - (3) Take part in church work.

21. If a young man leaves your Sunday school with a definite purpose to "serve God in his own village," is it an accident? Or has the Sunday school made definite provision to this end? If so, what provision?

MISSIONS

22. How may the sending of benevolence money to a denominational board, to be applied to a great campaign, be made to arouse world-wide sympathies and enthusiastic generosity?

23. What, on the other hand, are the advantages of applying contributions to the support of individual missionary workers? How is it possible to combine the advantages of both systems?

24. What bond exists in your community with some foreign land or home missionary field? (e.g., missionary or other person gone thither or foreigner or traveler come thence). Show in detail how you may use this link in the missionary education of your church.

25. Which have proved in your experience better adapted to arouse interest in missions, regular lessons in Sunday school, or children's missionary societies? Give instances and explanation.

26. What special advantages are presented by the concentrated work of a School of Missions lasting for several weeks? How may the interest aroused be carried over into the routine work of missionary societies and Sunday school lessons?

27. Describe suggestive applications of the following:
    (1) Talk by returned missionary.
    (2) Use of native costumes and curios.
    (3) Textbooks. (Give title and characteristics of each.)
    (4) Special room for Sunday school mission classes.
    (5) Special teacher for Sunday school mission classes.
    (6) Missionary plays and pageants.
    (7) Handwork.

To what age and to what sort of group (e.g., Sunday school class, children's society, etc.) is each method best adapted?

28. Describe methods of mission study devised by your own denomination for use with children. Take into account textbooks, outlines of work, plays, pageants, games, illustrated lectures, exhibits, etc. Which does your church need? What other means can be used?

29. Make a close estimate of the minutes spent annually in mission study by your Sunday school. What are the effects of this study? Is this a sufficient amount of time?

Chapter IV

WORK FOR AGE AND SEX GROUPS

I: Boys and Girls

Four out of five of the churches studied have each at least one organization for boys, one for girls, and one for both boys and girls. In this respect their situation is in marked contrast with that of the churches in 300 rural counties surveyed by the Interchurch World Movement, only one in twenty of which had such organizations.

RECREATIONAL AND SOCIAL ACTIVITIES

In their work for boys and girls, most of the churches studied endeavor, without discrimination or thought of return, to provide all children within reach with opportunity for wholesome recreation and social intercourse, for harmonious development of body, mind and character, and for religious training as well as for active service with the church.

The organizations include Boy and Girl Scouts, organized Sunday school classes, Intermediate Societies of Christian Endeavor, or similar groups. Form of organization has proved less important than program and leadership. Boys and girls are often banded in separate groups; but the activities for the two sexes though differing in detail are essentially alike. The fact, however, that many groups are following well known, clear-cut programs, such as that of the Boy and Girl Scouts, or that of the secondary department of the Sunday school, which are presented and explained in the literature of those organizations, obviates the necessity for any detailed description of their activities. Even churches that have not adopted scouting make use of certain scouting activities.

Athletics

An important part in the program is assigned to athletics. Indoor or playground baseball, volley ball, tennis, swimming, and basket ball are good games for church use, for several reasons. They can be played by the two sexes with the same equipment, either together or in alternating periods. All are inexpensive. All can be played out of doors; although basket ball is more of an indoor game. Only tennis and basket ball need specially prepared courts.

A church owning a gymnasium or having the use of a school gymnasium is able to conduct classes in gymnastics, and to make more extended use of indoor games in winter. Churches so equipped find it well to assign to the different age- and sex-groups certain afternoons or evenings of every week. In a number of the churches this work is under the charge of a salaried physical director. Though a director and expensive equipment are desirable, they are not essential, as the present emphasis of specialists in recreation is upon activities requiring no equipment.

Baseball League

For the boys, of course, the most attractive sport is baseball. The pastors of two of our churches who had organized their boys and young men into baseball teams, found it necessary to organize similar teams in other churches throughout their respective counties in order to provide contestants. The resulting baseball leagues have proved of great benefit to all organizations participating. In both cases, furthermore, they completely broke up Sunday baseball. In one case the organization of the league was made possible by the minister who, backed by a guarantee from his boys, persuaded the parents to give them Saturday half-holidays from farm work regularly in return for the abandonment of Sunday baseball.

Hiking

Another activity favored by church leaders is hiking. Hikes are something more than walks in the open; they have objectives, such as the study of geology or bird lore. The pastor of the Methodist Church at Bingham Canyon, Utah, the greatest copper camp in the world, uses hiking with unusual effect. The single, squalid street of the camp runs for thirteen miles through a narrow ravine without a single tree. At four in the morning the pastor arouses his scouts, that they may be ready to tramp two and a quarter miles through a tunnel before the movement of cars of ore begins. At the other end of the tunnel the boys come to a beautiful camp-site of the Methodist Epworth League, where they can study nature to their heart's content.[1] Hikes for boys and girls together have sometimes proved successful.

Coasting

In winter some churches provide facilities for coasting. Several own their own bobsleds, which are much in demand when the snow is on the ground.[2]

Rodeo

Out on the western slope of the Rockies the boys of the Collbran Congregational church have an annual junior rodeo, including a baseball game, a wild west show with real broncho busting, steer riding and horse racing.

Camping

At least five of the churches have camps. Camping is no longer a very costly enterprise. The Boy Scouts and the Y. M. C. A. furnish in pamphlet form many useful hints.

[1] See "Churches of Distinction in Town and Country," Chapter IV.
[2] Because one boys' club in a church not included in this study owned a bobsled and raced it against the boys of another church, two whole counties have come to have a bobsled league, the annual tournament of which draws hundreds of people from interested neighborhoods.

Men's Bible classes in several of these churches have undertaken to finance the enterprise at least in part. In one church the cost per boy is as low as $2.50 for two weeks. The church owns permanent camp equipment; and to reduce transportation expenses the boys are taken to the camp in automobiles.

In camp programs, an important part is given to athletics, particularly water sports, and to nature study. Discipline of the camp is easily maintained by the infliction of penalties for the infraction of rules. It is of the utmost importance to have a program and to keep it running on schedule time. The arrangement of the program is of less importance. For impressionable adolescents the free life in the open, the study of nature and woodcraft, the heart-to-heart talks around the camp fire in the evening, the mystery of the night as sleep closes about the camper—all these help to build character and to deepen Christian loyalty. Some of the leaders are volunteers. Some churches which do not maintain camps, send boys to county or regional camps of the Y. M. C. A. or of the Boy Scouts.

Vocational Training

The program is by no means exclusively one of physical activity. Several of the churches have weekly or fortnightly club meetings for organizations of both sexes. No feature of these meetings seems to be more appreciated by the youngsters than that relating to vocational guidance. The leader invites representatives of various professions and occupations to address the group. The lawyer, the doctor, the contractor, or if it be a girls' club, the teacher, the Home Demonstration Agent, the landscape gardener, or the nurse each talks to the group about his or her profession. The talk is followed by a general questioning of the speaker. On such occasions the boys and girls show unusual interest. The addresses supplement in an ideal way any vocational work that may be undertaken by the school.

Character Reading

Character reading has attracted to one minister, for an interview, virtually every boy and girl in his community. They have been intensely interested in what he has told them of themselves. Organized athletic activities are of very great value to a leader possessed of insight, in that they enable him to understand the characters of the boys and girls, which understanding may be put to good use in the effort to lead them to the great decision of the Christian life.

Other Activities

A number of these churches include in their programs provision for sex education.

Several churches, moreover, make effective use of training in music. One conducts an orchestra of seventeen pieces; several have bands. Others, under the leadership of professional musicians, have trained junior choirs, or choruses. One church has two choirs, one of children and one of young people. The young people sing each Sunday at the evening service. From the point of view of church leaders, work with musical groups has several peculiar advantages. The children develop a real love of music, and enjoy the practice hours. The group effort, by its curbing of the natural desire of the young to win personal approval, affords a training in teamwork of the utmost value. The singing for services, especially as this is ordered by liturgical churches, stimulates love of the church, and habits of church-going.

EDUCATIONAL ACTIVITIES

Agriculture

A number of the churches conduct educational activities adapted to the life of the boys and girls. Through church initiative, pig-clubs, calf-clubs, tomato-clubs, or canning-clubs are organized under the charge of the county agent or the home demonstration agent. The colored churches of the

Methodist Episcopal circuit near Gonzales, Texas, hold an annual exhibit of cotton, vegetables, fruit, and hogs raised by the boys and girls under the direction of the club leader. Prize winners are given a free trip to San Antonio. Through these exhibitions, the fathers are challenged to equal or improve upon the work of their children.

Simple courses are sometimes given in hygiene, nursing, and cooking.

Collections

Some of the churches take advantage of the normal interest of adolescents in collecting. It little matters at this age just what is collected, whether butterflies or arrow-heads or stamps. A wise leader can make good use educationally of this interest in collecting. Annual exhibits of collections can be made to focus the attention of the parents and the community upon what is being done.

Radio

Two of the boys' clubs in these churches have radio outfits. The boys and their friends gather in the clubroom at the church or at the community house to listen to the voices that come through the air.

The Clubroom

With boys' and girls' organizations, proprietorship in a special room means a great deal. Most of the churches having such facilities allow the different groups to express themselves in their own rooms by means of pictures and other decorations. Besides promoting a sense of ownership in the youngsters, this allows a group leader to cultivate habits of neatness in them and to teach them elementary principles of interior decoration. Boys and girls who feel that a part of a building is actually theirs are more inclined to respect the entire edifice.

SERVICE

Adolescents naturally receive more from the church than they can contribute in return; yet it is the experience of these churches that the boys and girls are eager to serve when they can. They help distribute the church papers. They aid in helping the sick and those in need. Since the boys of one community were organized by the church, a certain widow has never been obliged to chop a stick of wood. The boys also usher at the church services; though they doubtless prefer taking care of the stereopticon and other parts of the recreational equipment.

The Boy Scouts of the Presbyterian Church at Dayton, Indiana, form the Village Fire Department; they have charge of the apparatus and respond to all alarms, which are sounded on the village church bell. Their prompt work has checked more than one serious conflagration.

II: CHILDREN

Activities for younger children are almost entirely within the Sunday school or the Junior Christian Endeavor, and are simple in their nature. A large number of the churches have the children at morning worship for what is called a "Junior Sermon," and two have them fully organized according to the well-known Junior Congregation plan.[3]

Some organizations, among them the Queen Esthers and the King's Heralds, study interesting courses on missions and undertake their own definite part of the work of missions. Of seven children's groups so engaged, one supports an orphan at a mission school and one a bed at a hospital, while the others perform some similar service.

In each of several of the churches a monthly social for children is given over to simple games of various kinds. A successful experiment has been made at Centerton, Arkansas, with a "weekly hour of story-telling."

[3] The subject is further treated in the chapter on "Worship." See also "The Junior Congregation," Farrar. Published by Fleming H. Revell.

III: YOUNG PEOPLE'S ORGANIZATIONS

Most of the young people's organizations of these churches belong to the Christian Endeavor type, and include such denominational organizations as the Epworth League, the Luther League, and the Baptist Young People's Union. The young people's societies are kept by these churches for the young people alone. The younger married folk and those still older are absorbed by other organizations either in or out of the Sunday school.

The significant thing in connection with these young people's organizations is that they have so generally succeeded in working out their own relationship with the church school. The church school is specifically for religious education. Each class is a one-sex group. Even where there are graded lessons there is hardly any opportunity for the young people to express themselves. A teacher is in charge, over the teacher is a superintendent and then an organization, and the young people have little control.

In the young people's organizations, there is quite a different state of affairs. The sexes are not separated. Common problems are discussed. In the programs the leaders do not hesitate either to alter the topics or to give local application to the discussion. The national overhead organizations, such as the United Society of Christian Endeavor, help materially. They suggest numerous committees with very definite tasks and the ingenious young folk soon discover the necessary local adaptations. Through these they share in the missionary program as well as the local program. The methods and activities employed by all these organizations are too well known to require description.

SOCIAL ACTIVITIES

Socials and "sings" are of frequent occurrence, as are musicals, pageants, and more ambitious forms of dramatics. The Centerton Methodist Church has a chorus of fifty voices gathered from both village and country. The young people of two churches have produced operettas, both of which have been given by request in neighboring communities.

The plays frequently staged always prove popular and are sometimes repeated in places near-by. It is important that plays selected have educational value as well as that they be interesting enough to insure financial success.[4] Literary meetings are frequent, and debates that are keen and full of zest. On the programs appear such topics of practical or current interest as the European crises, the present economic situation in rural America, and the county Juvenile court in its relation to the prevention of crime.

A few societies are organized to pursue together some common interest, such as dramatics, music or photography. At Bingham Canyon, for instance, where the pastor found the young people going off on Sundays to take all sorts of pictures, many of which he knew they would some day be ashamed to own, he organized them as a Camera Club and taught them photography, including the making of lantern slides.

A number of the activities of the boys and girls already mentioned carry over into the program of young people's societies; for example, athletics, hiking and other outdoor activities. During the summer many young people's societies hold swimming socials.

Social and religious activities are happily combined at the Brick Presbyterian Church at Perry, New York. Groups of men, women, boys and girls use the recreation rooms, each group having a special night for its activities; and each month there are suppers, sometimes for separate groups and sometimes for several groups together. After the meal, which is never omitted except in case of absolute necessity, there is a religious discussion, usually led by an outsider, often by a minister, or the school superintendent. In 1922, three groups studied Fosdick's "The Meaning of Service." No pressure is needed to arouse interest. Following the discussion the group has the use of the recreation rooms

[4] Community Service, Inc., of New York City, will furnish a list of plays. Some denominational headquarters, especially those of the Episcopal and Presbyterian churches, can make excellent suggestions.

which are under the charge of a director, a former Y. M. C. A. over-seas man. The average attendance ranges from seventeen for the junior boys to fifty for the men.

SERVICE FOR THE CHURCH

Leadership

The greatest service rendered to the church by the young people is the leadership they exercise over the boys and girls. To supervise this matter some societies appoint committees. Orchestras of young people with musical ability play not only for the young people's meetings but at the Sunday school sessions, sometimes at the evening service, and at church socials or entertainments.

Frequently, too, the young people have assisted in a house-to-house survey of the community. In some parishes they give clerical assistance to the pastor, address letters to the members and secure advertisements for programs of entertainments or for the church paper. Frequently under the oversight of some older person they manage the church paper entirely.

In not a few instances they have been successful in evangelistic work among others of their own age. The stimulus for this work, however, has come, in each instance, from the pastor or some other experienced leader.

Conferences

The Christian Endeavor Societies of Collbran and Montrose, Colorado, conducted in 1921 a Western Slope Young People's Conference, attended by delegates from many churches in that region. The topic was "The Relation of the Young People to the Church." During the conference the Collbran society staged a religious play; and both organizations made it plain that the future leaders of the Church were alive to social and religious problems.

Young people's societies are responsible for a significant amount of community service. A number take charge of annual lecture courses. Dramatic and musical efforts, though their purpose is generally to raise money, make nevertheless a real contribution to community life. In two instances, societies have coöperated with membership drives of the Farm Bureau. At Centerton, Arkansas, the young people were active in an anti-fly campaign and paraded the town, advertising by effective pageantry the importance of sanitary precautions against disease.

Meeting an Unusual Opportunity

When hundreds of migrant harvest laborers flocked to Larned, Kansas, ten or twelve days before the wheat was ripe, the young people there helped to man a welfare room and every evening while the harvesters were waiting for work to begin gave musical and dramatic entertainments. They were able to do this because the four Epworth Leagues of the Larned Circuit had been conducting an excellent social and religious program in preparation for an annual booth festival. At this festival or fair there are always exhibits of farm and home products as well as games and amusements of various kinds, a track meet, a baseball game and other athletic contests. The proceeds are given to benevolent causes.

Value of Full Program

In these churches the young people's problem is not a serious one. It may not be said perhaps that they have solved the problem; but rather that in many of the communities there has been no young people's problem because the churches have conducted a program adapted to successive ages which has carried each individual through his full religious experience.

IV: SOCIETIES FOR MEN

About two-thirds of these successful churches have societies for men. This proportion is far above the average.
Only one in twenty of the rural churches in the twenty-five
typical counties with which comparisons have frequently
been made, had such organizations. In the successful
churches the activities of the men are not only responsive to
their own social needs, but are directed to helping the church,
and to serving the community. The organizations fall into
two classes: (1) The men's club, which may or may not
include in its work a certain amount of Bible study, and
(2) the men's organized Bible class of the church school,
which meets on Sundays for religious education and also
carries on a week-day program.

MEETINGS

The activities include meetings for debates on topics of
national or local interest; for lectures or addresses by outside speakers; and for dinners. In more than half the men's
organizations the belief prevails that dinners add to the
interest of the monthly meetings. In some churches these
dinners are served by one of the women's organizations,
which thereby enriches its own treasury. In two churches
they are served by the domestic science class of the high
school.

These dinners afford good opportunities for the discussing
of matters of community concern. Often an address is given
by the county agent or by some representative of the college
of agriculture. The school superintendent talks of the needs
of the local school. A member of the board of education
explains the school budget. A state Y. M. C. A. secretary
impresses upon the men their obligation to the boys. One of
their own number who has returned from a trip describes
conditions in some distant part of America or in a foreign
land.

One dinner each year is almost always a "Father and Son
Banquet." Some of the churches strengthen the feeling of

fellowship there established between the boys and the men
by occasional discussions, participated in by fathers and boys
under the auspices of the church school. These discussions
of course deal with the problems in which both groups are
interested. Where the organization has a room of its own
the men often play checkers, pool, billiards and other games.

SERVICE TO THE CHURCH

Once organized, men are no more backward than women
in helping with church business. One club was responsible
for part of the work, and for all the money needed, to adapt
the church basement to the purposes of a social program.
Another has laid new cement walks from the road to the
church. Others raise funds for the general work of the
congregations. Some of the projects for raising money,
such as concerts, lectures, entertainments and moving-picture shows, are also forms of community service. One class
arranged for an exhibit of local products. A number have
baseball teams which, besides furnishing funds for the class,
provide entertainment for those who look on, and recreation
for the participants. Teams are often under the auspices of
the athletic associations. Such an association at Sacaton has
a membership of seventy men, and a football team that has
become famous.

LARGER RELIGIOUS SERVICE

The "Home-like Church" of Prairie Grove, Arkansas,
has a Men's Bible Class which has grown from sixteen members to forty. Its motto is "My Brother and I." To each
of the members is assigned a particular task. For each of
six districts into which the community has been divided, a
club representative is appointed who introduces strangers
to the local church of their preferred denomination, or if
such a church be lacking, issues a cordial invitation in behalf
of the "Home-like Church."

REACHING AN ENTIRE COMMUNITY

The Congregational Brotherhood of Whiting, Iowa, not wishing to grow at the expense of other denominations, brought committees from all three churches into conference. Obtaining a list of all the men in the community, the joint committee assigned to the different churches all the men that had shown any denominational preference; the others they divided equally. The Congregational Brotherhood received the names of 240 members and prospects. The prospects were interviewed and cultivated; and all the 240 members and the prospects were arbitrarily divided into four teams, with a captain and a lieutenant assigned to each. A spirited contest between these teams was then conducted on the basis of attendance at the Sunday school sessions and at the monthly meetings of the Brotherhood. Progress was recorded on a chart outside the Men's Room. The contest not only brought fifty new members into the Congregational Brotherhood, but resulted in a similar club being formed by the Methodists. Two important by-products, so far as the Congregational church was concerned, were increased attendance and the addition of several new families to the membership.

In three communities the men have been particularly successful in evangelistic work, as evidenced either in personal work or services in remote school houses.[5]

In many of these churches, moreover, the men are prompt in responding to cases requiring local relief.

COMMUNITY SERVICE

Successful campaigns for new school houses have resulted from the discussions in three men's organizations. Many clubs assist in carrying on work for boys. One brought about the purchase of an athletic field, and a number have sent boys to camp for several weeks. Farmers' Institutes have been held by a number of these clubs, and still others coöperate with the various activities of the Farm Bureau.

[5] See Chapter I, "Evangelism."

Several provide community picnics, one of which, boasting a speaker, a dinner, a baseball game and an athletic contest, was attended by 600 to 1,000 persons. Two, ceasing to be merely church clubs, have come to include the men of the entire community. They are still, however, largely inspired and led by the church. One of these has active committees concerning themselves with institutions and fairs, marketing, roads, recreation, benevolences, publicity and membership.

CIVIC RIGHTEOUSNESS

The *esprit de corps* born of working shoulder to shoulder has been responsible for many significant political victories. In two instances, members of the men's club of the church were stationed in various parts of the community on election day to furnish information to voters and to interest them in performing their civic duties. One of the communities in consequence cast a 90 per cent. vote.

Many of these brotherhoods perform for church and community virile tasks of many kinds. This fact, taken together with the unusually large number of brotherhoods among the churches studied, makes it probable that to these organized groups of men is due in some measure the notable success of the churches.

V: SOCIETIES FOR WOMEN

Every one of the churches studied has at least one women's organization. The activities of these societies are neither so diverse nor so unusual, compared with the activities of corresponding societies in other churches, as are those of some of the other groups in these successful churches. Like most Ladies' Aid Societies for the past two hundred years, they concern themselves with the general housekeeping of their churches, with the repair and improvement of church property, and with missionary activities. Like some of their contemporaries, they have begun to enter the field of community service. Much of their energy they spend in earning money, which in the aggregate amounts to a large sum. They sew, quilt, and hold bazaars, suppers, and entertainments.

A few of these societies distinguish themselves by conducting these activities on a strictly business basis. Unlike the women whose minister figured out that their labor brought the church one and two-thirds cents an hour, they justly estimate the value of time and of materials and exact a just return for both.

Two societies have furnished meals, not with the idea of seeing how many different foods could be put upon the table at the same time, but with a regard to food values. Another society used the church land for a garden and sold the produce.[6]

An organization in a county-seat town maintains at a county fair a booth whose annual proceeds run into hundreds of dollars.

NURSERIES

A form of service of other than monetary value is carried on by the women's organizations of several congregations. They maintain nurseries in which babies and younger children can be left during church services. Sometimes younger women and sometimes one or two of the mothers care for these children and amuse them with kindergarten activities. Two churches supply cribs for infants. Surveys have shown that responsibility for the care of small children causes one-tenth of the non-attendance of women at church services, and that when the mother stays at home the rest of the family usually stays also. A church nursery makes it possible for everybody to attend church.

OTHER SERVICE TO THE CHURCH

The parish visiting, which is the women's task in a large number of churches, is, in a few cases, conducted through one of the women's organizations. A society at Parma,

[6] It has been the practice of several country churches not included in this investigation to sell produce of a church garden, in the form of canned vegetables, to city consumers, through the society of a city church. The canning of produce, whether from a church garden or from home gardens, serves as a demonstration of this industry.

Idaho, commandeers the cars of husbands and friends twice a year to take shut-ins to the church for special services.

WOMEN AND MISSIONS

The activities of the women's missionary societies need little description. Like similar organizations the country over, they support native workers on the field through stated collections, mite boxes, or paid entertainments; they pack missionary boxes or send canned goods to mission stations; and at their meetings they study textbooks on missions and listen to papers by members, or to addresses, sometimes from returned missionaries.

Some of the missionary organizations, however, have undertaken more unusual enterprises. Half a dozen or more, capitalizing the dramatic instinct particularly of younger people, are giving plays and pageants.

In some churches, one women's society combines both local and missionary interests. Mission study is carried on, or papers are read, while the members quilt or sew. In a small congregation this works for efficiency, since the same women usually make up both organizations. The plan is much more successful when local and missionary interests are both considered at each meeting than when these interests are considered singly at alternate meetings. The latter plan is apt to result in many absences from every other meeting.

SERVICE FOR THE COMMUNITY

A number of women's organizations sponsor a Chautauqua or a Lyceum Course or both. Moved to action by addresses on the subject, some women's organizations have undertaken work for the betterment of schools, for stricter observance of quarantine, and for regulations to safeguard the purity of milk. One society has brought about the employment of a community nurse, and another has contributed $20 a month during the school year to provide milk for under-nourished school children.

A Restroom

The Community Circle ·of the United Church at Garretsville, Ohio, has furnished in the basement of the church a large, comfortable room which is open at all times to the public. When the room was equipped, the women distributed through the Garretsville trade area the following attractive invitation:

TO OUT-OF-TOWN PEOPLE

Friends:
A restroom for your comfort and convenience is now awaiting you in the Social Rooms of the United Church of Garrettsville— warm in winter, cool in summer, comfortable chairs, drinking water, lavatories, light, and cordial welcome. Bring your lunch if you wish.

The United Church is very glad to freely offer its Social Rooms to the general public, and sincerely desires that large use be made of them. We hope you will repay us by coming.

COMMUNITY CIRCLE COMMITTEE

In this restroom the Community Circle holds its regular meeting, as does the Mothers' Club of Garretsville.

The Ladies' Aid Society of Honey Creek, Wisconsin, has been for years one of the most influential factors in community well-being. It has organized, among other things, a Civic Club the object of which is to beautify the town.

Missions at Home

A piece of effective community service which is also missionary work of a high type, is rendered by the women of the church at Imperial, California, to the local Mexican women. One of the church women was chosen as a social service worker. On her committee, besides other women of the church, was a trained worker engaged by the Superintendent of Schools to teach the Mexicans and to work among them out of school hours. As the plan worked out the Mexican women were taken to the parish house on Friday afternoons in the school busses, and about a dozen were enrolled in various classes. Women of the church taught them sewing and other domestic arts. The director of the choir gave them instruction in English. Each week, church women served refreshments. At first the Mexicans were shy, but they soon became acquainted and friendly. Toward the end of the year the W. C. T. U., whose members had been asked to become Big Sisters to the Mexican women, invited them and their husbands to the high school for an entertainment, which was followed by games and refreshments.

With a few exceptions, these women's societies are engaged in the kinds of work that have long been familiar. Either because their earlier start may already have enabled them to standardize their methods, or because women are conservative, their organized work in the churches that have been studied, presents fewer features of striking originality than does the work of the men.

SUMMARY

Some of the activities possible for various age- and sex-groups are given below.

BOYS AND GIRLS

Athletics, including baseball, basket ball and volley ball, tennis, swimming, etc.
Hiking, with definite objectives.
Coasting.
Class in gymnastics.
Scouting.
Annual Camp.
Vocational guidance.
Character reading.
Sex education.
Collections.
Radio.
Orchestra.
Band.
Junior Choir.
Special club in church, assisting pastor as directed.
Coöperation with Farm Bureau in various production clubs.

CHILDREN

Junior congregation or children's service, sometimes in connection with regular Sunday morning service.

Monthly socials.

Weekly story-telling hour.

YOUNG PEOPLE

Many of the activities listed under boys and girls apply also to young people. Others are:

Weekly religious meeting.

Socials.

Sings.

Musicals, concerts.

Dramatic, including missionary pageants and plays involving character analysis.

Debates, discussions, addresses.

Leadership in boys' and girls' work.

Assistance in program of church when called upon by pastor.

Coöperation with school, farm bureau, and other community organizations.

MEN

Game and reading room.

Debates and forums.

Lectures.

Dinners.

Coöperation in boys' work.

Service to the church through raising money and making improvements to property.

Community service through concerts, Chautauquas, moving pictures, community picnics.

Organized athletics, especially baseball.

Evangelistic activities.

Welcoming and locating newcomers.

Local charitable relief.

Electing Christians to public office.

WOMEN

Raising money through sewing, quilting, bazaars, sales, etc.

Utilizing meals as domestic science exhibitions served.

Maintaining nursery at church during morning or special services.

Support of native worker on mission field.

Raising money for missions.

Mission study.

Guaranteeing a Lyceum Course or Chautauqua.

Bringing shut-ins to special services.
Providing outside speakers on missionary and local topics.
Work toward better schools, quarantine observance, pure food.
Maintaining a restroom.
Service to foreign-speaking groups.
Parish visiting.

BIBLIOGRAPHY

The Efficient Layman, or, The Religious Training of Men.— HENRY F. COPE. Griffith and Rowland Press, 1911. 244 pp.

Church Officers—F. A. AGAR. Revell, 1918. $.75. 91 pp.

Help These Women—F. A. AGAR. Revell, 1917. $.75. 83 pp.

The Ladies' Aid Manual—ROBERT E. SMITH. Abingdon Press, 1911. $.50. 72 pp.

Five Hundred Ways to Help Your Church—THERESA WOLL-COTT. Sunday School Times Co., 1912. $1.00. 364 pp.

The Boy and the Church—EUGENE C. FOSTER. Sunday School Times Co., 1909. $.75.

Boy Behavior—W. H. BURGER. Association Press, 1919. $1.25. 108 pp.

Leaders of Girls—CLARA ESPEY. Abingdon Press, 1915. $1.25. 216 pp.

The American Country Girl—MARTHA FOOTE CROSS. Stokes, N. Y., 1915. $2.50. 367 pp.

Serving the Neighborhood—RALPH FELTON. Missionary Education Movement, N. Y. $.75. 153 pp.

Ice Breaker and the Ice Breaker Herself—EDITH GEISLER. Woman's Press, 1921. $1.35. 163 pp.

Games for Home, School and Playground—JESSIE BANCROFT. Macmillan, 1922. $3.00. 556 pp.

Handbook for Workers with Young People—J. V. THOMPSON. Abingdon Press. $1.50.

The Boy Scout Movement Applied by the Church—NORMAN E. RICHARDSON and ORMOND E. LOOMIS. Scribner, 1915. $2.00. 445 pp.

Literature may be obtained from:

International Committee, Y. M. C. A., County Work Department, 347 Madison Avenue, N. Y. C.

National Board, Y. W. C. A., Town and Country Work Department, 600 Lexington Avenue, N. Y. C.

Boy Scouts of America, 200 Fifth Avenue, N. Y. C.

Girl Scouts, 189 Lexington Avenue, N. Y. C.

Woodcraft League, 13 West 29th Street, N. Y. C.

TOPICS FOR DISCUSSION

1. What specific things can a society of men contribute to the well-being of a church that, in the absence of such an organization, would be left undone or be performed less effectively?

2. List the aspects of community life that have been improved by one or another of the men's clubs described in this chapter or in "Country Churches of Distinction." Which of these matters need improvement in your community?

3. Compare the kinds of service undertaken by men's and by women's church societies. Do you see a specialization of function that works to the advantage of the church?

4. Has the higher education of women, and the wider activity of many women in welfare organizations and political life, lessened or enlightened and intensified the work of women in connection with churches? Support your opinion by reference to specific instances.

5. What are the relative advantages of (1) separate societies for home and foreign missions, and (2) a single society in the interests of both?

6. Describe methods within your experience by which, through church societies, young people have been trained to leadership.

7. How may young people's societies like the Christian Endeavor and Epworth League guard against the danger of emphasizing expression through speech rather than through character and conduct?

8. Explain the value of *esprit de corps*. How may this spirit be promoted by healthy rivalry among the various church societies?

9. Are middle-aged people in a young people's society a help or a hindrance? Explain.

10. "We should probably find that the junior and intermediate societies could easily attain all their ends in a Sunday school properly organized and managed."[1] Discuss this opinion.

11. What factors in the ideals and activities of the Boy Scouts fit this organization to the use of church workers?

12. What traits and accomplishments are essential, and what are desirable, in the leader of a boys' club?—of a girls' club?

[1] "Education in Religion and Morals," George E. Coe, Revell, 1909, p. 319.

13. "Young people should be given 80 per cent. of what they think they want, and 20 per cent. of what their elders think is good for them." Defend the principle involved. How, if at all, would you change the proportion?

14. What peculiar opportunities have musical groups, that is, the bands, orchestras and choir, as means of (1) molding character, (2) binding the members to the church, (3) serving the church as a group?

15. What should be the attitude of the church toward Sunday ball games?

16. "My young people," said a certain pastor, "are going to dance somewhere. To let them do so in the church vestry would cause unfortunate talk. I let them dance in the parsonage, where I can control conditions, and I play for them myself." Is this minister right or wrong, and why?

Chapter V

THE PLANT AND ITS EQUIPMENT

An enlarging idea of the function of the Church has caused congregations in these successful churches to modify existing plants either as to use or as to structure and then to erect additions, or new buildings, with rooms specially adapted for the adequate performance of the complex religious program of today.

But some of these vigorous organizations are still in the early stages of development; and, with respect to five or six of them, all work has to be done in one room or in one room and a basement. These churches make better use of poor plants than many others make of adequate ones. The Methodist Episcopal Church at Bingham Canyon, Utah, for example, which has only one small, poorly equipped room for social activities, nevertheless conducts a live program for every day in the year. The full use of what is available holds out the best promise of eventual extension.

This chapter, therefore, is not intended as a compendium on church buildings and equipment. It merely records the progress of these churches in obtaining, despite many handicaps, a material equipment sufficient to help them realize their spiritual ideals.

EXTERNAL APPEARANCE

The newer buildings possessed by these churches combine the distinctive features of church architecture with an appearance of adaptability to service. Each is designed to be in keeping with the physical characteristics of its site, and with the style of neighboring buildings. They are set in ample grounds; their lawns are graded and often planted with shrubbery. They suggest by their appearance the ideals for which it is the mission of a church to stand. Said the surveyor of one of them, "The brick and stucco walls have simple dignity; and the whole building seems to say 'come in.'"

The average cost of the church plants of these successful churches, together with the parsonages and community houses when the plants include these, was $30,418. The average cost of the church plants of the twenty-five counties surveyed by the Interchurch World Movement and resurveyed by the Committee on Social and Religious Surveys, was $6,048.

AUDITORIUM

The most important room in the church building is, of course, the main auditorium. In the larger plants its appearance is properly suggestive of its use for religious services. There is no gaudy frescoing and the coloring is in soft tones. The indirect system of electric lighting provides a diffused illumination without glare. Real care has been exercised in planning the seating arrangements. One or two churches have opera chairs, but the majority have retained the time-honored pews. Pews or chairs are so placed as to insure a maximum of comfort; and their color and design have been made to harmonize with the general scheme. In buildings where the main auditorium must be used for many different purposes, some of these features have necessarily been sacrificed for practical ends. The tendency has been, however, to reserve the main auditorium exclusively for worship or for worship and for meetings whose main feature is either music or speaking.

PROVIDING FOR THE SUNDAY SCHOOL

Planning for the accommodation of the church school is an important problem, especially as the school in a successful church is apt to grow even more rapidly than the congregation and to overflow the plant. In the rural churches the best plan has been to build, along the sides of the main auditorium, classrooms which may be opened into it. Such an arrangement makes it possible not only for the school to assemble in its entirety but for an overflow attendance to be accommodated at church services. An architect can easily adapt rooms so placed to the general scheme of a church building.

A small church whose Sunday school meets only in the main auditorium or in one assembly room in the basement, has, of course, a more difficult problem. As a rule, a church with a large building, especially a single-story one, distributes its Sunday school rooms all through the building. One has constructed a mezzanine floor which is given over entirely to classrooms. Others have placed rooms behind the pulpit alcove and organ. The slight addition to the length of the building occasioned by this arrangement allows for the inclusion of still larger rooms on the floor above. On week-days these additional rooms, wherever placed, can be put to many other uses.

THE BASEMENT

The location of the church school in the basement is not to be recommended. A church organization about to erect a building ought not to plan for this arrangement unless the land lies so that the basement may stand far enough out of the ground to allow for sufficient light and ventilation. The larger churches have utilized their basements for heating plants, for storage, for gymnasium purposes and occasionally for rooms for the Scouts or for a few Sunday school classes. Many a small congregation, however, finds in an existing basement the first outlet for an expanding program. During sessions of the church school, folding doors or curtains, even of such light material as burlap, afford classes some degree of seclusion. When these curtains or partitions are put back against the wall or run into their grooves, the room is once more available for social purposes.

The Wayland Christian Church at Gresham, Nebraska, which is in a small open country neighborhood that is unlikely ever to grow very much, affords an example of the skillful utilization of a basement. This basement was forty feet long and thirty-two feet wide. An areaway of considerable size at each window changed the apartment into a reasonably bright and cheerful one. At one end a kitchen was constructed; at the other a stage with curtains suspended from wire rods. Below the stage was a place to store folding chairs. Curtains provided means of dividing the space into six classrooms for the use of the school on Sunday.

SPACE AND EQUIPMENT FOR COMMUNITY SERVICE

Community service has a real place in the program of these churches, though it is incidental to their other activities. The adapting of their plants to various community uses, including recreation, has presented little difficulty. Rooms used on Sunday for organized classes are clubrooms, game-rooms, or reading-rooms during the week. Restrooms open on holidays to farmer's wives, and where country families may even eat their luncheons, become on Sundays nurseries and kindergartens where mothers wishing to attend services may leave their babies in the care of trustworthy persons.

Much of the community program is carried on in the basement or the community house. The Brick Presbyterian Church at Perry, New York, has in its basement a kitchen, a serving-room, and five recreation rooms which are provided with reading matter and games. The equipment includes two bowling alleys (the best in the town), a pool table, a cue-rocque table (primarily for boys and girls under fifteen but used by persons of all ages), a shuffle board, and provision for table baseball and half a dozen smaller games.

THE KITCHEN

A kitchen has become so generally recognized as an important part of the social equipment of a church that it is not surprising to find that each of thirty-four of the church plants has one. In some instances advice regarding equipment has been given by the Home Economics Department of the college of agriculture of the state, and in one or two cases by the county Home Demonstration Agent. There has been effort to make the kitchen a model one. Tables, range, sink, and cupboard have been so placed as to make for the highest degree of efficiency and the fewest possible steps for the worker. In some cases sinks have been built in, and draining boards have been made ample for the number of dishes to be cared for. To remove danger of waiters bumping into one another at church suppers, with resulting breakage of dishes, most of the kitchens have two serving windows, one for outgoing and one for incoming trays.

The kitchen equipment is surprisingly complete. In the church at Parma there is a modern electric range instead of the rusty old stove usually provided for the women's societies; and the same church has a hot-water heater. Another church has a five-gallon electric coffee-maker. The churches are well stocked with china; one has in its cupboards six dozen of everything needed for the tables. Often too the china is of attractive design and adds to the effectiveness of tables set for a banquet. In some cases it is marked, as is the glassware as well as the silverware, with the initials of the church, which occasionally lends this part of its equipment to less fortunate organizations. The equipment also includes such necessary articles as soap-shakers, can-openers, measuring-cups, and other devices that make for efficiency in the kitchen.

Kitchen utensils are sometimes acquired through a kitchen-shower. The women of one church had a supply of articles they wanted placed in a store window and people chose their gifts from these. As a result articles not needed were not included among the gifts.

THE STAGE

In the programs of a dozen of the churches considerable prominence is given to amateur theatricals. One, with hardly any equipment, places screens of various colors, heights, and designs across one end of the Sunday school as a stage setting. Another has built a good platform, upon which the pulpit is placed on Sunday. A properly constructed stage may become a gallery from which an audience may watch a basket ball game on the floor below; and should be large enough for use by an orchestra during Sunday school sessions. Painted scenery and drops of expensive material are unnecessary. For both front drop and background, excellent substitutes for these may be made of gray canton flannel. This costs little, is of neutral color, does not soil easily and falls in graceful folds. With proper lighting and carefully selected stage furniture, it can be made to create the desired illusion. To avoid embarrassment to amateur Thespians trying to rid themselves of make-up after a performance, a certain church has running water in dressing-rooms at the end of the stage.

OTHER DETAILS

The rooms in the buildings of these churches are all as serviceable as they can possibly be. Just as the lessons in the church school are graded to suit the ages of the pupils, so the chairs are graded to suit the size. Pictures and coat-hooks are placed low for the use of the smaller children. The Methodist Episcopal Church at Cimarron, New Mexico, has a checkroom for hats and coats. It also has a social-room with soft green hangings, reed tables, easy-chairs, and shaded lights, making it not only attractive but a model of good taste. A model in its way also is the room for the girls at Parma, with its blue and brown floor, its leather couch and its attractive wicker chairs. More than one of these churches has grouped rooms around a fireplace to give the homelike atmosphere of a living-room or the cozy effect of a woodman's cabin. And effects of this kind are worth far more than their small additional cost, which is easily met when the interested church organizations provide the equipment for their own rooms.

Both the success of these churches in arranging for details and the few mistakes which some of them have made, lead to the recommendation that a congregation ought not to go far with any plans for building or remodeling a church without consulting experts. Not many small-town architects are likely to be informed regarding all the features of a comfortable and efficient church plant. To their aid can be summoned the experts of the architectural bureau of the denomination; and workers from the state college of agriculture will advise concerning such matters as grounds, interior decoration, and the kitchen. In nothing is expert advice more needed than in the selection of the church organ and the heating plant.

GYMNASIUM AND COMMUNITY HOUSE

Nearly half the churches have gymnasiums. Some of these are in separate community houses, some under the same roof as the auditorium for worship. In a number of instances the gymnasium of the week day is the church school room of the Sunday; and this is not a bad adaptation. The minimum equipment for a gymnasium is inexpensive and useful. A pair of basket ball goals can be attached to backing boards of the proper size and erected on poles by volunteer labor. A volley ball with net can be purchased for less than $10. This game, too little known, is suited to both sexes and almost all ages. Another useful game involving little expense is indoor baseball. Even with the minimum of athletic equipment a great deal can be accomplished, especially if there are local leaders to conduct gymnastics not requiring the use of apparatus. The equipment can be indefinitely expanded. Suitable mats are needed with some apparatus and for wrestling; but with these begin the larger costs. It would be better at first to install shower baths, lest overheated children leave the building without taking proper precautions for putting their bodies in normal condition.

The experience of these churches proves that a community house is not beyond the reach of even a small church. Two of the smallest and poorest of the group own such buildings. True, these structures are not expensive; they have been contrived in each case out of a combination store and dwelling. The one at Shuford, Mississippi, which is emphatically in the class of "less favored" agricultural communities, contains a hall and four other rooms. The hall is being fitted up as a gymnasium-auditorium, with facilities for community meetings, musicals, and indoor athletics. Another room will serve as a library and sitting-room; another as a kitchen; still another, a large apartment, as dining room. The last is to be a nursery to which the mothers may bring their babies. Canoga, New York, is another village below the average in economic status which has yet been able to add to its church plant an effective community hall.[2]

At Lander, Pennsylvania, a little village of 500 inhabitants six miles from a railroad, a Methodist Episcopal church has added to its one-room building a two-story "ell" to be used as a community house. Here it was not only possible to have a gymnasium-auditorium, but to house in separate classrooms several departments of the church school. Where there is a community house, it almost invariably houses the town library, if there be one, or packages of books from the State Library Commission.

At the other extreme from the simple community houses already described is the Lanier Boys' Club building of Grace Methodist Episcopal church at Spencer, Iowa, which includes a gymnasium with a complete line of apparatus, and which is connected by an underground passage with a swimming pool.

STEREOPTICON

Three-fourths of the churches have stereopticons. These they find invaluable not only for purposes of recreation but for use in giving instruction. The stereopticon has become an established feature of the equipment of the average church. All necessary information concerning makes and prices can be obtained through denominational boards or from the advertising columns of most religious periodicals. The churches in this group obtain their slides either from the denominational boards or from various state agencies, par-

---

[2] For a description of the Canoga plant see "Churches of Distinction in Town and Country," Chapter III.

ticularly from state library commissions and state colleges of agriculture.

MOVING-PICTURE MACHINE

More than a quarter of the churches studied own moving-picture machines. The moving-picture, as an instrument of religious work, is winning its way more slowly than the stereopticon; but none of the churches using one would be without it. Two or three machines of excellent make are obtainable. Advice as to which is best in any given case may be obtained from the local moving-picture operator or from the extension department of the state university.

Cost of Machine

Machines of a number of makes can be purchased for from $400 to $550; and as most of these are fireproof, they may be used without booths, provided the proper authorities are given opportunity to test them thoroughly. It is necessary, however, that they be submitted to this test and that the fire insurance agent who handles the policy of the church be notified in order that the proper underwriter's permit for showing pictures may be obtained.

Program

The machines are used for various purposes. Most of the churches do not hesitate to show, on Sunday evenings, films picturing incidents from the Bible, or such pictures as "The Stream of Life," "Modern Samaritans," and the like. The picture, when used for evening service, is almost always preceded or followed by a short talk by the pastor, and is often made a part of a religious service.

At community meetings, or gatherings for recreation, such educational or entertaining films are shown as "Our Daily Bread," "The Land of Cotton," "Consolidated Schools" or "Gravel Road Construction." Of all the churches studied, the Methodist Episcopal church at Rolla, Missouri, had the finest selection of general pictures. They included last year:

> "Miles Standish."
> "The Last of the Mohicans."
> "Mistress of Shenstone."
> "Ann of Green Gables."
> "Daddy Longlegs."
> "Les Misérables."
> "Evangeline."
> "Turn of the Road."
> "The Servant in the House."
> "Shepherd of the Hills."
> "Little Women."
> Various Tarkington comedies.

Cost of Service

The cost of film service varies with location. A church in a county-seat on the main line of a railroad has to pay far more for its films than one miles back in the mountains, or on the prairie, which does not enter into competition with moving-picture houses. Virtually all these churches, however, and many others, have found it possible to pay for the machine with the profits from a number of week-night entertainments; after which either pictures may be shown at cost or the proceeds may be utilized for other purposes. A film from a commercial distributor seldom costs a church more than $50; and a large number of good films can be obtained for from $5 to $20 each, plus transportation expenses.

Sources of Films

Of almost a score of organizations which at present furnish films to churches, all have been employed by one or another of our group of churches. A number of concerns, commercial in character but serving only non-theatrical organizations, include the International Church Film Service, the Sacred Film Corporation in America, Community Motion Picture Bureau, and others. All these companies, too, have been utilized by at least one of our churches.

These churches also obtain films from commercial distributors who have been brought to understand the situation and who send only suitable material. The Famous Players Lasky Corporation, controlling Paramount Pictures, has a non-theatrical department for churches, schools, and community organizations which furnishes excellent films such as "The Old Homestead" and "The Little Minister." Similar departments either have been organized or are being organized by several other commercial distributors.

Certain state universities, state libraries, and similar public agencies send out on circuits to schools, churches, and community organizations excellent films at charges sufficient only to cover expenses.

In a number of cases a church that does not own a moving-picture machine has the use of one belonging to a school; and two churches obtain them at commercial moving-picture theatres. One church has agreed not to purchase a machine so long as the quality of entertainment offered by the theatre in the community continues to be good; and another has promised to refrain from showing pictures on Sunday evenings so long as the village moving-picture theatre is closed on that evening.

DEFINITE BUILDING PLANS

Perhaps it should be repeated that a single chapter on this subject cannot be expected to cover the entire question of church erection and equipment. It ought, however, to draw attention to certain definite situations and to present concrete examples of what these churches do. Three plans are therefore submitted here to make clear some of the points covered in this chapter. The first is that of the Southern Methodist Church of Centerton, Arkansas, in the foothills of the Ozark Mountains—the plan of a new building. The second is that of the Congregational Church at Collbran, Colorado, representing the church as it has been rebuilt and enlarged to meet the demands of community service. The third, that of the Presbyterian church of Parma, Idaho,

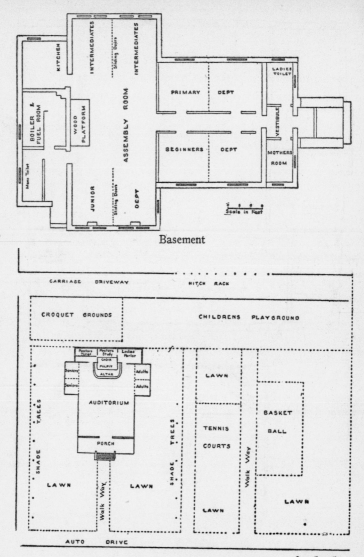

Basement

Main Floor

FLOOR PLANS OF COMMUNITY CHURCH AT CENTERTON, ARKANSAS

100

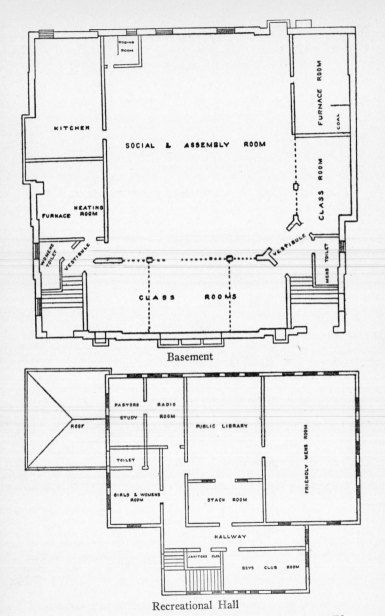

Basement

Recreational Hall

FLOOR PLANS OF FIRST PRESBYTERIAN CHURCH, PARMA, IDAHO

101

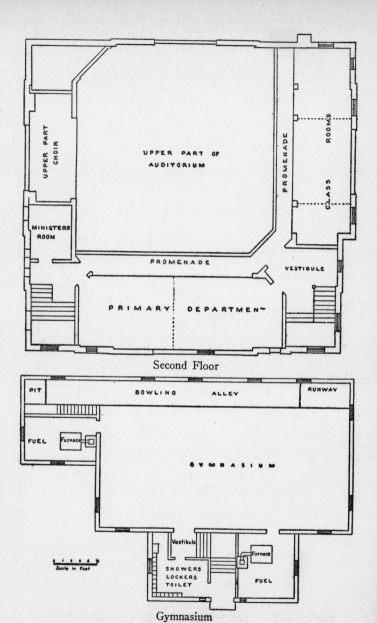

Second Floor

Gymnasium

FLOOR PLANS OF FIRST PRESBYTERIAN CHURCH, PARMA, IDAHO

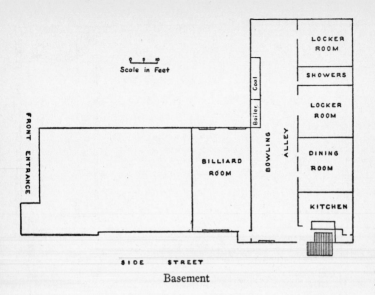

Basement

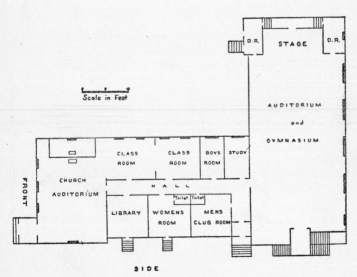

Main Floor

FLOOR PLANS OF CONGREGATIONAL CHURCH, COLLBRAN, COLORADO

103

represents the best plant possessed by any of the churches studied with the possible exception of the Methodist Episcopal church at Spencer, Iowa.

CENTERTON

The plans of Centerton well illustrate the use of rooms on either side of the main auditorium and at the rear of the pulpit; also the use of the basement for an assembly room with a stage.

The plan of the main floor is self-explanatory. The side rooms, which during the study period of the Sunday school accommodate some of the classes, may at will be thrown into the main auditorium. Because these rooms extend only part way toward the entrance, the building approaches in its architecture the cruciform type; but the unusual advantage possessed by this particular church is that the pulpit may be seen from virtually every point in any of the rooms. The basement, besides allowing for utilities, provides separate rooms for some departments of the Sunday school. The assembly room on the basement floor is to be used for athletics. The height is adequate, but the length and breadth are hardly sufficient for basket ball. Another objectionable feature is the use of the two columns which support the girder running across the middle of the ceiling. It is possible to support such girders without columns, which not only obstruct floor space but add an unnecessary element of peril during indoor athletics. An interesting feature of this basement is a mothers'-room.

The most uncommon feature in connection with the church is to be found in the layout of the grounds. Set far back from the street, it has a generous expanse of lawn and plenty of shade trees. A large space to the right of the building is to be used for tennis courts, croquet grounds, children's playground, and basket ball court. With an equipment like this and a climate such as that of Centerton, the handicaps of the basement will not prove so serious as in the cases of churches farther north or west.

COLLBRAN

The basement plan of the church at Collbran illustrates a commendable utilization of what was a single-cell church plant. The building as now constructed is in the shape of an L. The church auditorium, facing the street, is practically removed from the recreational activities. In the addition there are classrooms for the Sunday school on either side of a hall between the auditorium for worship and a gymnasium. The gymnasium is used not only for athletics but for entertainments, fairs, institutes, and similar functions. The stage, which is at one end, is provided with a dressing room at either side. This part of the building has a separate entrance so that those assembling for social activities need not pass through the church auditorium.

PARMA

Community House

The plant at Parma consists of a beautiful church building and an attractive and useful community house. The plans need little explanation. The gymnasium is large enough for any kind of winter athletics and is provided with shower baths and locker-rooms. Along one side is a bowling alley, and over it is a gallery for spectators. On the second floor is a radio-room, a reading-room and clubrooms for boys and girls. Part of this story is open to the roof, which is provided with skylights.

SUMMARY

Certain observations are true of all these buildings.
1. The edifice is attractive, and the grounds are well kept.
2. The auditorium suggests in design and decoration its use for church purposes.
3. The church school is provided with suitable facilities, including classrooms, whenever possible, and provision for separating different groups by the use of curtains.
4. There are facilities for community service. Where there are classrooms, these are used during the week by organizations. The basement, a wing of the church or a

separate parish building houses the cultural and recreational program.

5. All available space is used to the maximum.
6. Equipment is up to date. The kitchen is a model of arrangement and furnishings; chairs are comfortable; heating, lighting and sanitation are efficient. There is regard for utility, comfort and dignity.
7. The use of the stereopticon and the moving-picture machine is increasing.

BIBLIOGRAPHY

Adapting the Church Building for the Purposes of Religious Education—Bulletin No. 5, Presbyterian Board of Publication and Sabbath School Work, 1922, Philadelphia.

Planning Church Buildings—HENRY E. TRALLE. The Judson Press, Philadelphia, 1921. 162 pp. $1.25.

Progressive Suggestions for Planning Church Buildings—E. M. CONOVER. The Home Missions Council, New York, 1923. $.50.

Better Rural Church Houses—FRANK G. DILLARD. Bureau of Architecture, Methodist Episcopal Church, Philadelphia and Chicago, 1921. 24 pp. $.25.

The New Country Church Building—EDMUND DES. BRUNNER. The Missionary Education Movement, New York. 141 pp. $.75.

The Moving Picture and the Church—ROY SMITH. Abingdon Press. $.35.

Motion Pictures: The Experience of One Church—GEORGE E. BEVANS. Board of Home Missions, New York. $.05.

Any church contemplating the erection of a community house or gymnasium should not fail to get one of the handbooks on gymnasium construction and equipment, published by such concerns as Spaldings or the Narragansett Machine Company of Providence, R. I. The books published by these firms, particularly by the latter, are extremely suggestive. They may be obtained either directly or through a sporting goods dealer.

TOPICS FOR DISCUSSION

1. "Many great leaders of the Protestant churches are today debating whether the modern church should be in the style of an office building or in the style of a cathedral." [3] State

[3] "The Future of the Churches," R. W. Babson, p. 59.

the case in favor of each of these types of church architecture.

2. "Its equipment is for a church what its factory building and its machinery are for a manufacturing establishment."[4] Considering the open country church as comparable to a factory, tell (1) what it should produce, (2) what rooms and equipment are therefore requisite.

3. "If the churches are to have a brilliant future, they must capitalize art and music in some worth-while, practical way."[5] How may the church building "capitalize art"?

4. A certain church has a gingerbread style of trimming, gaudy windows, and on the platform a bowl of paper flowers of clashing hues. Even if these things truly express the taste in the congregation, is it right to gratify this taste in the church building?

5. Explain the psychological basis for the view held as early as the days of the apostles, that it is a function of the Church to "serve tables." What does the proper performance of this function make requisite in the church building?

6. Give instances of church buildings in which features that make for efficiency are combined with those inspiring beauty; and explain as fully as possible how in each case the double aim was attained.

7. There were in the U. S., in 1916, 203,432 buildings used for worship. Church edifices are exempt from taxation. Some persons feel that the public ought to have the use of all this untaxed property for a longer time than a few hours a week. How can the church plant be equipped to serve the community a greater part of the time?

8. "Get the spindle and distaff ready, and the Lord will supply the flax." Should this motto be applied to church equipment? That is, shall a church with a "one-celled" building start on a new career by erecting an elaborate edifice with many classrooms, a kitchen, a dining-room, and a gymnasium? Or should it begin by entering upon work for its community and build only when there is imperative need?

9. A church has received a legacy to be used either for the purchase of an electric motor, a pipe organ, or a moving-picture machine. What conditions should determine the choice?

[4] Shailer, Mathews, "Scientific Management in the Churches," p. 53.
[5] R. W. Babson, Ibid., p. 59.

10. State several reasons for equipping a church plant with clubrooms.
11. Write specifications for a new building, or for enlargement of the present building, which will enable your own church to fulfill its mission to the community.

MOVING-PICTURES

12. Many people in a certain village prefer cowboy pictures to any others. To what extent should their taste be decisive in choosing the films presented?
13. Would it be advisable to have moving-pictures in your community on Sunday evening? Explain.
14. Should moving-pictures be given in the church auditorium in any circumstances? Give reasons for or against this course.
15. A certain village has a commercial moving-picture show that presents films not only trashy but questionable. Point out several courses that might be adopted by a church or a ministerial association to combat the evil.
16. Let each student name any films which churches have used or might use with good results, giving, when possible, the name of the agency from which each picture may be obtained.
17. How may moving-pictures be so used as to prevent the audience from tiring of them?

Chapter VI

CHURCH FINANCE

Not one of the churches studied is without a system for conducting its finances; and not one fails to operate that system with vigor and efficiency. As a result they secure without difficulty the funds required to defray the cost of their extensive programs.

BUDGET

In every case the governing body of the church, after a careful study of the receipts and expenditures of the past year and of the requirements and the program for the year to come, determines upon a budget. As a rule, this budget covers all local expenditures, sometimes including the maintenance of the church school. In a few instances, however, there is a separate budget for the recreational activities or for the expenses connected with a community house; and in two cases there is a separate budget for missionary offerings.

PREPARATION FOR THE EVERY-MEMBER CANVASS

Almost all the churches conduct annually an every-member canvass. After the budget has been determined, those in charge appoint a date for the financial campaign, and begin to prepare the members of the congregation for the making of their contributions or pledges. Everything possible is done to inform the constituency of the church's needs. The pastor discusses the budget in the meeting of his Council, and the members of the Council representing church societies report upon it to their respective organizations. A circular letter is distributed to all the members of the church, and often where the church is alone in the field to all the families in the community.

These letters clearly and impersonally state the case for the church. There is no scolding, no begging, no cajoling in them. They ask contributions on the basis of service to the community and to the world-wide interests of the church.

CAMPAIGN PUBLICITY

The budget is published and explained in the parish paper, if there is one. Often, too, topics relating to stewardship are treated in one or more sermons from the pulpit. Talks on the budget are, in several cases, given at services by laymen. Two churches have used to good effect a play published by the Missionary Education Movement, entitled "The Canvasser and Mr. Brown."

Some churches employ what amounts to display advertising in their parish papers, in dodgers, or as headlines for the letter of appeal. Thus the Presbyterian church at Canoga, New York, began its statement as follows:

It Is Coming!
WHAT?
Our Annual
Every Member Canvass
WHEN?
Next Week, February 9th to 11th.
Kindly be at Home.
Motto: *"Every Person Giving Something Every Week."*

Toward the end appeared this appeal:

When this letter reaches you, stop and think—What would Canoga be without a church? What would you do without it? What would your wife and children do without it? In the light of these things decide what you will do so that when you are approached next week you may cheer the solicitors with a generous response.

The letter used in 1922 by the Union Congregational Church at Montrose, Colorado, gave for each day in the week the average number of persons using the community building during the preceding six weeks, the total showing an average weekly attendance of 2,907.

You may readily see [the letter continued] that it means both work and expense to take care of more than 2,000 people per week. It will take $175 per week to underwrite this budget.

$175 Per Week—This Will Do It

10 persons giving $3.		per week............	$ 30.00
15 " " 2. " "			30.00
30 " " 1. " "			30.00
100 " " .50 " "			50.00
120 " " .25 " "			30.00
Loose offering			5.00

$175.00

All who contribute $25 or more to the general budget shall be given a gymnasium ticket for the year 1922.

Besides distributing circular letters, the Community Church at Parma, Idaho, published in a local paper an article called "What the Budget Means." This article began:

Not a single cent has been included in the budget that is not essential to the continuance of the Community Church enterprise. It seems high at first thought, but let us see what it means to the community.

Numbered paragraphs then presented in some detail ten contributions made by the church to the common life. These were in brief: Religious services; church building open for any public meeting; dining-room at the disposal of the community; community house; gymnasium; shower baths; auditorium; quarters for public library; beautiful grounds, and institutional activities. Each paragraph ended with a question, such as: "Would you want to be without it?" The article concludes:

If you believe these ten things are worth while, do your full part toward next year's budget. The canvass is Sunday afternoon at 2 P. M. If you prefer, mail a check to W. E. Babcoks, treasurer.

Giving the treasurer's name at the end is particularly effective. Reprints of this article were distributed at the church.

THE CANVASS

After such preparation as this comes the canvass, usually made on a Sunday afternoon, by the men of the parish going out in pairs. The number of teams varies from a dozen to as many as twenty-two. These men, of course, have been thoroughly instructed concerning the items of the budget, so that they can answer questions. Such coaching the church at Collbran accomplishes at a banquet. It is impressed upon the men that they are rendering a service vital to the cause of God and the Church. Every effort is made to gain interviews with every one, even at the cost of a second or a third visit. Characteristic of the prevailing spirit of thoroughness is the following extract from a set of instructions used in a cattle-raising country: "Get a subscription from each member of the family. If they cannot give cash they may give a calf or something else."

The canvassers for several churches emphasize the fact that the budget covers the funds needed during the coming year for the entire work of the church, including on the one hand all benevolences and assessments, and on the other all items of local expense; so that if the budget is covered, the church program can be carried into operation for the year without further appeal. In some cases, they also explain that the church treasurer will remit money to any denominational board desired.

Teams are usually assigned to districts of the parish. Occasionally, canvassers are allotted persons with whom they have influence. The calls are brief and businesslike and often prove agreeable both to guests and to hosts. At a number of places the church office is open through the afternoon to receive returns, and at the evening service at least a partial report is always presented. The names of persons not found are assigned to other canvassers, who call during the week. By the following Sunday, as a rule, the task has been completed.

An interesting variation of this method has been tried at Grace Church, Spencer, Iowa, where the stewards were stationed at tables in the church before and after services to receive subscriptions. Other churches hold what is called a volunteer day, in order to lessen the work of the can-vassers by letting those who wish to do so subscribe volun-tarily. For some of the churches the budget has been oversubscribed.

A small number of the churches, instead of conducting an every-member canvass, raise their funds by other meth-ods equally systematic. Not one of them lives from hand to mouth, by passing the hat or by selling chicken-pie and ice-cream at less than cost.

Assessments

At New Monmouth, New Jersey, the members of a Baptist congregation gather to make their pledges at what is called an Annual Roll Call. The Lutheran church at Stanton, Iowa, with more than 1,000 members and a budget of more than $23,000, raises all its money through indi-vidual assessments upon members. A financial committee of twelve men divides the entire communicant list into groups. Those in the first group are assessed $5 a year each; those in the second group $10 each, and so on up to groups of those assessed $50 each. Every one accepts his quota as a matter of course and makes the payments either annually or semi-annually. The treasurer, who is a bank president, keeps his books at the bank; and thither the people go to pay their church dues, as in some places they go to pay for gas, water or telephone service.

Tithing

A few churches use the method of tithing. Of the members of the Southern Methodist church at Prairie Grove, Arkansas, 40 per cent. are tithers. At the Memorial Presbyterian Church at Dayton, Indiana, a Tither's League of twenty-one men contributes a little over one-fourth of the total amount received. One objection to tithing is that it is seldom adopted by the entire church membership.

PER CAPITA EXPENDITURE

The amounts contributed, though in the aggregate considerable, are usually made up of many subscriptions not individually large. In Perry, New York, for example, though the congregation is wealthy and the annual budget amounts to over $8,000, few subscribers contribute more than $5 per week. At Stanton, Iowa, as has been implied, the quotas set by the Finance Committee do not in any case exceed $50 a year.

Where there is a large building program the annual per capita expenditure per resident member is above the normal. Building programs bring marked but probably temporary spurts in per capita giving. The ranchers of the Baptist rural parish at Arnold, Nebraska, who live in straitened circumstances, are contributing an average of $42.97 a year per resident member. At Cimarron, New Mexico, the average contribution is $70.24. The average annual contribution per *active* member for the 1,046 churches covered in the typical counties surveyed by the Committee on Social and Religious Surveys in 1920 was $15.69. These contributions include, of course, those of churches with building campaigns. The contributions, per *resident* member, of those of the successful churches now being studied averaged $19.93. The larger membership, and the support from outsiders attracted by the work of these churches, as well as from members, make possible the financing of an extended program on per capita expenditure little above the average.

A number of these churches collect special offerings at such times as Christmas and Easter, in addition to the subscriptions gained through the every-member canvass. The Brick Presbyterian Church of Perry, New York, reserves from $500 to $600 a year of the denominational benevolence quota to be raised at Christmas time.

Sometimes these special offerings apply toward the support of the church's foreign pastor. More often workers supported on the foreign field, usually native evangelists, are cared for by subordinate organizations. Considerable sums are often raised for this purpose which do not pass through the hands of the church treasurer. Grace Methodist Episcopal Church at Spencer, Iowa, for example, not only supports nineteen native workers but the missionary superintendent of Meerut, India, whose name appears on service bulletins as "Pastor Abroad." The church at Dayton, Indiana, likewise, pays half the salary of a missionary who is referred to as its "Foreign Pastor." On a smaller scale the support of workers is undertaken by other churches or by their organizations, especially by societies of women or young people. The money thus applied is sent to the denominational board, sometimes through the church treasurer, sometimes directly from a society. Such contributions for special workers are allowed to count on assessments.

DENOMINATIONAL CAMPAIGNS

The far-reaching campaigns of the various church bodies —such as the New Era Movement, the Baptist Forward Movement, and the Centenary—with their inspiring purposes, their definite objectives and time limits, and their remarkably telling publicity, combined with the pressure put upon each local church to meet an augmented quota—have effected for the churches studied, as well as for live churches in general, a considerable increase in denominational benevolences. In more than a few cases, benevolences have increased from two to five times as fast as has even the rapidly growing total of disbursements. The church at Davis, California, for example, raised its contribution to denominational purposes from $40 in 1912 to $868 in 1922; and last year it over-subscribed its quota by 20 per cent. In the past three years, the Presbyterian church at Middle Octoraro, Pennsylvania, has applied to benevolences a sum equal to the total amount contributed in the preceding fifteen years.

THE FOLLOW-UP

The best of budgets and the most thorough every-member canvass will not be of great value unless subscriptions are paid. These churches have little difficulty with their follow-up. The money pledged is usually paid in weekly installments through the use of the duplex envelope. .

In many cases treasurers mail, to all subscribers, quarterly statements of account. Often each of these is accompanied by a communication such as that employed at Parma, Idaho, which is as follows:

Enclosed you will find an exact duplicate of your account on the treasurer's books. If you are paid up, accept this as a receipt with appreciation. If your account is in arrears, will you not pay up promptly as the church has no other means of support?

These quarterly statements, with occasional reminders from the pulpit or through a church paper, seem to furnish all the persuasion necessary. As a matter of fact, the best follow-up of these churches is afforded by their many-sided programs, with the accompanying publicity. People know that failure to pay means injury to a program justified in their eyes by its service to individuals, to the community, and to the Kingdom of Heaven.

AMOUNT AND APPORTIONMENT OF EXPENDITURES

The average amount raised annually by these churches, exclusive of mission stations, is $4,900. This sum is more than three times as large as the average for the twenty-five typical counties, which was found to be only $1,445. The amounts raised by many of the churches, moreover, were well above the average for the group; and the largest budget of all, as has been said, amounted to more than $23,000.

In considering the distribution of these large amounts, it is necessary to remember that many of these churches under inquiry support large programs either of building or of community service; and that all pay the larger salary required by a resident minister. Even so, the part of the total devoted to benevolence was, on an average, 26 per cent., surprisingly near to the 30.4 per cent. for the twenty-five typical counties. This average, moreover, was considerably exceeded by some of the churches; and two reached the high figure of more than 42 per cent.

The portion of the budget of the successful churches which was applied to salary of minister was 33.9 per cent., a figure noticeably lower than the average for the typical counties, where though only about half the churches had resident ministers, 41 per cent. of the total expenditure was for salary. The church with the largest budget applies only 10.6 per cent. to salary of minister. This ratio is comparatively low owing, of course, not to niggardliness, but to the large scale of the operations.

DEBTS

Over a dozen of the churches are in debt in amounts varying from less than $100 to $15,000. In most cases the debts were incurred for extensive building operations. Like a business firm or a school board, the churches accept debt as a natural part of their financial operations. Most of them have made arrangements for repaying the loans either through a sinking fund provided for in the budget; by pledges which are to run for a series of years; or in other legitimate ways. One church, for example, is making payments on its building out of the receipts from moving-picture shows. Debt is not incurred, however, at the end of a year in order to make up a deficit in the current expense account.

HOME MISSION AID

Fifteen of the churches, that is to say, three in every eight, receive home mission aid. The ratio is about twice as high as was found to prevail in more than two hundred counties subjected to special study. The large proportion of aided churches results naturally from the attempt to include among the communities studied at least one representing each special type of rural home mission need. In many of these communities, such as one in the open country in the cotton belt, or a mining town with a large foreign element, a church could hardly attain notable success in the absence of aid from a church board.

In each of a number of cases, money was appropriated by the board to enable a church to seize what is called by one denomination a "strategic service opportunity." Thus churches at Sacaton, Arizona, San Gabriel, California, and Buckhorn, Kentucky, are conducted as mission stations, serving respectively Indians, Mexicans and southern mountaineers. Others, such as those at Collbran and Cimarron, are each at the center of a wide area standing to the church as a larger parish, the evangelization of which is financed in part with home-missionary money. Of still others, each is assuming for the first time a heavy program of community service; while there are some which are being conducted as demonstration parishes, to guide and inspire other churches of the denomination that lie in the same area. No doubt all of these last named will eventually come to self-support.

This statement in regard to home mission aid is limited to grants made for salaries and general maintenance expenses. It does not include grants made to five of these churches for buildings. Denominational boards dealing with church erection make outright grants under certain conditions to local congregations needing new equipment. These are not continuing grants to be renewed annually, but each of them represents a completed transaction. They should not, therefore, be confused with appropriations made by home mission agencies for the continuing support of a field,

which, in the usage of most denominations, are annually
renewable for as long a period as conditions warrant.

In some instances, because of peculiar local conditions,
the grant must be indefinitely continued: at Bingham Canyon, for example, the constantly shifting population of a
rough mining camp is not likely ever to support a greatly
needed religious ministry. But with some such exceptions,
the aid is given to help a weak church become strong enough
in time to meet successfully and unaided the test of a great
opportunity. In many instances the money has been granted
in regularly decreasing amounts for a stated period of five
or six years. Few of the aided congregations have received
help long. Some of them are rapidly approaching self-
support; one, in fact, which was aided last year, is able this
year to stand alone. It is reassuring to find that churches
so weak as to require home mission aid have been able, with
its help and with the leadership it ensures, to make such
progress and to perform such notable service as to justify
their inclusion in this group of successful churches.

FINANCING THE SUNDAY SCHOOL

The maintenance of the church school is included by seven
of the churches in their budget; in the other cases the schools
are supported from their own weekly offerings. The running expenses vary from less than $100 to $448. The
average annual cost per pupil is $1.18. Six schools with
more than 300 pupils are conducted more economically, at
an annual cost per pupil of $1.00. The six schools with
fewer than 100 pupils each have, on the other hand, the still
lower cost of $0.92 per pupil; but this is due presumably to
their making less adequate provision for work. The highest
cost per pupil is $2.15; and the next highest, for what is
perhaps the most efficient of all the schools, is $1.95.

STEWARDSHIP TRAINING

Both the members and the young people of these churches
are trained in the habit of giving. Reference has already
been made to measures connected with the canvass. Pro-

vision for training in stewardship is in many cases provided throughout the year for all groups, beginning with the Sunday school. At the Methodist Episcopal church of Lander, Pennsylvania, a large proportion of the Sunday school members took part in 1921 in a reading course in stewardship ending with a contest. Denominational textbooks are studied by Sunday school classes or other study groups. In some instances the maintenance of the Sunday school by the church is designed to instill habits of giving through the presentation of all offerings to benevolences, especially to missions.

In other cases schools pay their own expenses and learn thereby to bear responsibility for the support of religious work. Several schools have a budget, one item of which is applied to the running expenses or to the building program of the church. Sometimes money is voted by the school to a neighboring hospital or to local relief. Letters from missionary representatives of the church or of the special organization are read before the Sunday school or missionary society to bring home the fact that contributions actually produce results on the field. A number of the churches distribute the effective literature provided by denominational boards. For example, the St. Mary's Reformed Church at Silver Run, Maryland, distributed a denominational questionnaire on tithing, and later discussed it at a meeting. Stewardship, again, is the concern of one of the eight departments of the Community Church at Imperial, California.

The churches studied have, in brief, a well-rounded financial program. Beginning with a budget, they raise the necessary funds through every-member canvass or other systematic procedure, and distribute them with due regard to the claims of both work at home and the Kingdom through the world. Generosity is cultivated and justified through constant emphasis upon the duty of Christian giving.

SUMMARY

Some of the essentials of a good financial system as determined by the experience of these churches are:

A carefully prepared budget.

Thorough explanation of the budget to the membership and constituency by publicity, discussion and sermon.

An every-member canvass or some other system to reach the entire membership.

A careful, continuing follow-up.

Stewardship training in Sunday school and church.

BIBLIOGRAPHY

Modern Church Finance, Its Principles and Practice—ALBERT F. McGARRAH. Revell, 1916. 328 pp. $1.25.
Church Finance and Social Ethics—FRANCIS J. McCONNELL. Macmillan, 1920. 130 pp. $1.50.

TOPICS FOR DISCUSSION

1. "The spiritual welfare of a church is closely related to its financial self-respect."[1] Is this true? Just how does "financial self-respect" promote "spiritual welfare"?

2. Does an annual canvass tend to distribute the financial support of church work more generally throughout the membership and the community?

3. Which of the methods of raising money described in this chapter would in your judgment be efficacious for the church with which you are most familiar? Why?

4. Are special offerings at Christmas and Easter—
   (1) The expression, in psychologically desirable action, of the feelings stimulated by these festivals; or
   (2) Unworthy attempts to make capital of, for example, the Christmas spirit?

5. Do church fairs and suppers make the "Father's house a house of merchandise"? Or can such methods of raising money be justified on grounds of (1) financial stress, (2) by better social life and recreation?

6. "The more money I put into my farm, the more I get out. It's the same way with a church." Give arguments for or against this familiar assertion.

7. A church gives $150 to foreign missions, while receiving $200 home mission aid. Is this state of things justifiable? If so, how?

[1] "The Church and Country Life," edited by Dr. Paul L. Vogt.

8. "The vital religion of a church will grow with its generosity. Even the weaker church should have some share in the world-wide work of missions and should strive to meet its apportionment, adopting it definitely as a part of its regular budget." [2] Discuss the pros and cons of this opinion.

[2] "The Church and Country Life," edited by Dr. Paul L. Vogt.

Chapter VII

ORGANIZING THE CHURCH FOR THE PROGRAM

From early Colonial days until recently, all Protestant churches in America, whatever their denomination, had in respect to organization certain characteristics in common. Local authority was vested in the congregation, which met at least annually. Responsible to the congregation were two boards, one charged with authority in material matters, the other having to do with spiritual affairs. The members of these boards were known as stewards, trustees, elders and deacons. The two groups were seldom coördinated. In addition to the pastor, the organist, and the janitor, there were usually two other officers, a clerk or secretary, and a treasurer. Even this minimum organization was simplified in some cases by a single board having both spiritual and material tasks assigned to it. Many churches had two subordinate organizations, the Sunday school and the Ladies' Aid Society, over the work of which the official boards seldom if ever exercised any supervision. Terms of office were usually long, and officers often grew very old and conservative in service. Long ago the accepted duties of both boards became stereotyped.

But in late years there has been a marked change. Denominational overhead organizations have become far more aggressive, and have set tasks and fixed quotas for the local church. Spurred by the strengthening hold of new interests upon the time and energy of its members, the Church has developed new enterprises and undertaken new tasks partly in the way of self-preservation. Moreover, the social gospel has been widely preached, and has been carried more and more into practice. Finally, denominational campaigns and the example of modern business have set the Church new standards of efficiency.

In the two generations within which the change has come, church organization has greatly increased in complexity. Development has been chiefly along three lines. The first change was in the formation of additional societies to perform new functions. The missionary awakening of the early Nineteenth Century, for instance, resulted in the formation in the local church of women's missionary societies. Half a century later came the spread of societies for young people, and then the extension of the system of special organizations to other age- and sex-groups. The usual number of such organizations in the churches studied is from four to seven. Five congregations have from nine to thirteen.

A second development was evidenced by the appointment of committees to care for each need as it might arise. The members of the committees have been selected from the different parts of the parish, so that people of each neighborhood might be brought into relation with every interest of the church.

Later the people of any neighborhood who served on the different committees were organized into a local group committee. This third form of development, which has come to be known as the unit or group system, has been extensively promoted by denominational agencies.

The committee form of organization is largely concerned with the internal working of the church. Two churches, each with many committees, have assigned to them the following interests: ushers, finance, estimating minister's salary, parsonage and furniture, fuel, music, benevolences, Sunday school, auditing, church records, gymnasium, etc. One of these churches has a total of thirty-two committees and sub-committees. Each of two small colored churches has sixteen committees, in one or the other of which is enlisted a representative of almost every family.

In the second place, some of the committees supervise such organizations as the Sunday school and the young people's society. Such supervision presents difficulties, unless, as in the churches in question, the committees are made up of persons vitally interested in the organization concerned. Organizations and committees alike ought to be supervised by one or the other of the official boards. Finally, the committee system is apt to fail in presenting a comprehensive, carefully balanced program.

Where the committee system is carefully coördinated with the program and is well administered, it has real value. Several churches that use it successfully have avoided the dangers of lack of balance and of overemphasis on local needs. The Community Church of Imperial, California, has eight so-called departments, with a membership range of from four to ten. These cover spiritual resources, religious education, social service, gospel extension, publicity, finance, music, and stewardship. The gospel extension department is responsible for the conducting of the Sunday schools and for preaching services at five outlying points. The chief task of the department of social service is Americanization work among Mexicans. The religious educational department, in addition to supervising the home Sunday school, conducts the annual School of Missions. The department of spiritual resources, composed of the pastor and the elders, has oversight of evangelistic campaigns and of all personal work. Three of the chairmen are women. Every department holds a business meeting once a month.

The Memorial Presbyterian Church of Dayton, Indiana, uses the same system with virtually the same departments. It has, however, a department of every-member mobilization, the duties of which are to assign to every active member some definite task, to keep individual records, and to award suitable recognition for services. The department of gospel extension coöperates with all boards of the denomination except that of foreign missions. The department of spiritual resources is responsible for increasing attendance, for promoting family worship in homes and for organizing and directing bands of personal workers. This church makes a practise of assigning to the same department men and their wives.

The departmental system in use in three of the forty churches differs from the committee system, of which it is a recent outgrowth, in not being an accidental aggregation of separate teams but the result of a deliberate endeavor to make due provision for all parts of a well-balanced program devoted not only to internal affairs but to the larger interests of the community and the Kingdom.

The use of committees or departments does not necessarily do away with societies. The church at Dayton, for instance, with eight departments, has also eight organizations. Moreover the districting of the parish and the use of committees are often combined in one system, as has been pointed out; and there may be districting not in combination with the committees, even when the same church employs both systems, as is the case both at Dayton and at Imperial. The multiplication of committees has been accompanied in some cases by an increase in the number of church officers. For example, the Methodist Episcopal church at Randolph, Iowa, has not only seven committees, but ten trustees, thirty-four stewards, and sixteen other officers.

This more complex organization, extreme examples of which have been cited, makes it necessary for the official boards responsible to the congregation to be kept fully informed as to all church activities; and for the various agencies to be made to function smoothly in a single well-rounded program.

THE PASTOR'S COUNCIL

Sometimes these ends are accomplished by the creation of a pastor's council or Cabinet, composed perhaps of one member from each of the official boards, the president or secretary of each organization, and sometimes, if either exists, the heads of departments or the chairman of the group leaders.

This Cabinet becomes the right arm of the pastor, and meets at least monthly or on call. It has four principal functions. Primarily it is concerned with coördination. At its meetings the program of the church as a whole is discussed, as well as the part to be played by each organization. It clears up misunderstandings between organizations. No society may schedule any event without consultation with the Cabinet. The representatives of the official boards, being in constant touch with all developments, become interpreters to their colleagues of all activities. In one case the board representatives have the power of veto over all decisions.

The Pastor's Council is also the central agency through which in any exigency the minister can get his plans before all the other agencies. In some churches, prior to the every-member canvass, this Council holds a meeting at which the budget is explained, after which the representatives of the other organizations explain it to their constituencies. A similar course is followed at the time of the adoption of the annual program. The recommendation of each representative to his society is conclusive because it has behind it the decision of the Cabinet.

A third important function of the Pastor's Council is the initiation of plans. To it may be proposed new projects favored by any board or society. The ensuing discussions reveal the positions of all elements in the church on all proposals. Because it is representative of so many interests, the Council's measures are generally well considered and its recommendations favorably received by the congregation.

Finally, the Pastor's Cabinet makes it possible to correlate the suggestions of the various national or sectional overhead organizations. The advice upon work for adolescents given to one church by the state officers of the Sunday School Association, and that of the Christian Endeavor Society, contained more than 50 per cent. of duplication. The suggestions in themselves were admirable; but just how they were to be carried into effect by local organizations could be decided only when the entire local situation was understood.

Of the forty churches, the one that best combines several methods into one is perhaps the Presbyterian church at Parma, Idaho. This church has eleven subordinate organizations besides the Sunday school. The parish, moreover, is divided into nineteen districts, within each of which are several group leaders, one of them serving as chairman. The duties of these group leaders are to visit people in the district, especially newcomers, upon whom they report to the pastor; to make persons acquainted with one another; to report changes of residence and cases of misunderstanding in church matters; and to announce forthcoming church events. They have also responsibilities in connection with the semi-annual surveys and with the evangelistic campaign. With the nineteen chairmen the pastor holds periodic consultations. An Executive Council includes the chairman of the group leaders, the pastor as representative of the Session, and the head of each organization, as well as extra representatives from important divisions of the Sunday school.

The overhead advisory body of some churches is so large as to be cumbrous and to constitute sometimes a clique within the church. Occasionally, too, the presence of three or four groups of teams, organized in accordance with different systems, causes too great a complication of machinery. The three systems are most effectively combined when the societies perform the greater part of the work under the general supervision of departments or committees, and when the units of the parish are used almost exclusively for evangelistic effort and volunteer parish visiting.

As has already been implied, these churches have definite programs. In half of them the first step toward the building of a program has been a survey.

THE SURVEYS

These churches recognize the dependence of their work on thorough knowledge. Many of them have conducted community surveys, and three undertake to keep their information up to date by restudying the community either every year or every six months. The surveys have varied from a simple house-to-house religious census to a careful analysis of the church and the community in relation to each other. The studies have sometimes been conducted under the leadership of the minister, by either the Sunday school teachers, the group leaders, or the young people.[1] In all the most ambitious undertakings the minister himself has joined actively in survey work.

[1] One definite illustration of the work of men's Bible classes in such surveys is noted on p. 79.

Parish Map

After the survey has been made a map of the parish is drawn. It is useful to include in the map every home in the area, and to indicate the church affiliations of the residents. There are many simple devices for this based chiefly on the use of different colors for different denominations. One of the best is the parish chart of M. C. Bishop, which can be obtained by writing to Mr. Bishop at LaCrosse, Indiana.

Records

A valuable adjunct to the church survey map is a card index of the membership and constituency. The cards required may be obtained from denominational or undenominational publishing houses, or they can be ruled by the minister himself and placed in a home-made box-file. On a simple 3 x 5 card there is plenty of space for the family address, the names and birthdays of all members of the household, their membership in the church and its organizations, the church offices they may have held, and the status of each as to marriage, dismissal, and the like. On the back of the card can be kept a record of pastoral calls. A church having sole responsibility for an entire community should have a card for every household.

In several communities with more than one church, the survey and mapping of the parish were undertaken coöperatively.

PROGRAM

When the results of the survey have been tabulated and interpreted and the parish has been mapped, the whole matter is considered by the official boards of the church and, where such a thing exists, by the Pastor's Cabinet. Those in charge then construct, in the light of the survey findings, one of the most important things in the work of the church —its program. Where there is a Cabinet, that body discusses the part to be taken by every church agency in carrying out the program. In some cases, where there is no

Cabinet, each organization makes its own program, and these are assembled into a unit which is presented by the minister to the congregation at its annual business meeting.

How a survey may result in a program enlisting all church agencies is well illustrated by the example of the Community Church of Imperial, California. The survey disclosed within the trade and school community a large unevangelized area containing 2,100 people with virtually no religious affiliations. At a so-called "Set-Up Meeting" preceded by a dinner, the findings of this survey were presented by the pastor to the whole congregation; and to meet the needs revealed a broad program of church activities, to be divided among eight departments, was outlined and enthusiastically adopted. Thereupon a "Covenant of Worship and Service" was distributed, thus giving every one an immediate opportunity to volunteer for some phase of the new work. For the gospel extension activities alone the number of volunteers was fifty. This survey and the meeting following it have become annual institutions.

Many of the churches have constructed their programs, at least as far as the more important undertakings are concerned, for more than one year. Whether for a year or for a longer period, the program keeps a goal before the church whose progress then may be definitely marked. When it has adopted a clear-cut program to which every individual and organization in the church is geared, it knows where it is going and it is on the way.

Typical of these programs are the two that follow. One of them, at Collbran, Colorado, is in two sections. The first of these deals with the year directly ahead, and the second with objectives for a period of four years. The former exemplifies the departmental type of organization, showing the parts taken by the various groups and societies. The two programs together suggest that the year of a successful church has pretty constant features. It includes a Rally Day—sometimes two—a financial campaign, an evangelistic campaign, and the celebration of the great festivals of the Church and of the nation.

UNIFIED CHURCH PROGRAM FOR 1922-23

Church Motto for all departments: "Seek ye first His Kingdom and His Righteousness; and all these things shall be added unto you." Matt. vi, 33.

I. Program for Department of Social Service:
  1. Promote young people's organizations
     Boy Scouts
     Camp Fire Girls
     Christian Endeavor, Junior and Intermediate
     Societies
     Sunday school.
  2. Sustain Community House Activities
     Library
     Game Room
     Men's Club
     Ladies' Work.
  3. Provide Entertainment
     Weekly moving pictures
     Home talent plays
     Debates
     Forum.
  4. Develop Extension Activities
     Movies in outlying schoolhouses and churches
     C. E. meetings in outlying schoolhouses and churches
     Children's Hours in outlying districts.

II. Program for Department of Religious Education:
  1. Emphasize responsibility of religious education committee
  2. Through preaching, teach all truth regarding the Ideal Commonwealth of the Kingdom of God
  3. In the church school organize teacher training school
  4. Hold Summer School of Religious Instruction: Collbran Plan
  5. Encourage reading of library books on the Kingdom of God
  6. In C. E. and all other organizations further study of the Kingdom
  7. Stress to limit religious education through the local press.

III. Program for the Department of Missions:
  1. Have study group on "Modern Conquests of the Kingdom"

2. Have every society give to missions
3. Have the church meet its benevolence quota in full
4. Have the church select a particular mission field as its own and the American Board assign a missionary representative as ours
5. Instruct in work of Fred White, worker supported by this church, in Florence, Alabama
6. Provide books and literature on missions
7. Cultivate the missionary committee.

IV. Program for Department of "Worship and Fellowship":
  1. Develop reverence in worship through Children's Church, in C. E., in adult worship
  2. Stress the "Practice of Life in the Kingdom," learning to live together in a relationship which continues forever
  3. Emphasize worship through music
  4. Stress Bible study and prayer
  5. Cultivate fellowship through socials and emphasize on goodwill.

V. Program for Department of Evangelism:
  1. Special drive until Easter for commitments to the Christian life
  2. Maintain evangelistic effort through religious education, through personal work, through literature, through mass evangelism, and pulpit utterance
  3. Seek to avoid leakage in adolescent age.

VI. Program for Department of Business:
  1. Advance work on church manual; prepare constitution in 1922
  2. Organize church; elect deaconate, board of trustees
  3. Adopt (a) duplex envelope system, (b) weekly payments to church and for benevolences
  4. Work for beautifying of church grounds, and improvements such as a cement walk in front of the church.

THE FOUR-YEAR PROGRAM

1922–23 Religious Education stressed: "Kingdom of God" central idea.

1923–24 Social Service stressed: Survey made and program made according to needs revealed.

1924–25 World Christianity stressed: Review of world situation made, study of societies for world work, etc.

1925–26 Spiritual Quickening stressed: Emphasis on personal
religion and evangelism through religious education,
personal evangelism and mass evangelism.

At Silver Anniversary present souvenir pamphlet containing
history of church, its organization, its membership, its constitution (in brief, a complete manual).

The second program, that of the Methodist church of
Randolph, Iowa, presents the events of the ensuing year,
grouped according to the organization in charge. This
arrangement conduces to the proportionate sharing of labor,
and to the sense of responsibility. Certain other churches
publish their programs in order of dates, an arrangement
that is perhaps more convenient for reference.

CHURCH CALENDAR
1922

Ladies' Aid Society:

Feb.	1, Wed.	Father–Son–Big-Brother Banquet.
Apr.	15, Sat.	Easter Sale and Banquet.
May	13, Sat.	Annual Banquet, Epworth League.
Aug.	23, Wed.	Membership Rally.
Sept.	6, Wed.	Reception for Sunset Club.
Oct.	15, Sun.	Harvest Home Dinner.
Oct.	20, Fri.	Reception for Official Board.
Nov.	4, Sat.	Colonial Supper.
Dec.	6, Sat.	Annual Supper and Bazaar.
Dec.	27, Wed.	Annual Social Meeting.

Sunday School:

Apr.	16, Sun.	Easter Program.
June	11, Sun.	Children's Day.
Aug.	1, Tues.	Sunday School Picnic.
Sept.	12, Tues.	Annual Meeting.
Sept.	24, Sun.	Promotion Sunday.
Oct.	22, Sun.	Rally Day.
Dec.	24, Sun.	Christmas Program.

Children's Socials:

Feb.	11, Sat.	Valentine Social.
Mar.	18, Sat.	St. Patrick's Social.
May	6, Sat.	May Day Festival.
Aug.	26, Sat.	Lawn Party.
Oct.	28, Sat.	Hallowe'en Social.

Union Meetings:

May 21, Sun.	Baccalaureate Services.
May 28, Sun.	Memorial Sunday.
Nov. 30, Thur.	Thanksgiving Services.

Women's Home Missionary Society:

Jan. 27, Fri.	Annual Program, Queen Esthers.
Mar. 2, Thur.	Mite Box Opening.
June 5, Mon.	Annual Meeting, Queen Esthers.
June 15, Thur.	Mother-Daughter Meeting.
Sept. 7, Thur.	Annual Meeting.
Oct. 5, Thur.	Reception for Families.

Epworth League:

Jan. 12, Thur.	Baseball Tournament.
Feb. 9, Thur.	Baseball Tournament.
Feb. 13, Mon.	Valentine Social.
Mar. 17, Fri.	St. Patrick's Social.
Apr. 1, Sat.	All Fools' Day.
Apr. 16, Sun.	Easter Morning Watch Service.
May 13, Sat.	Annual Banquet.
May 14, Sun.	Anniversary Service.
June 19, Sun.	College Night Services.
June 23, Fri.	Ice Cream Social.
July 4, Tues.	Fourth of July Picnic.
Sept. 1, Fri.	Fall Reception.
Sept. 10, Sun.	Rally Day.
Oct. 31, Tues.	Hallowe'en Social.
Dec. 24, Sun.	Christmas Program.
Dec. 29, Fri.	Home-Coming Rally.

Church:

Feb. 1, Wed.	Father–Son–Big-Brother Banquet.
Feb. 16, Thur.	Men's Reception for Ladies.
Apr. 16, Sun.	Easter.
May 14, Sun.	Mothers' Day.
June 14, Wed.	Flag Day.
June 25, Sun.	Automobile Sunday.
July 2, Sun.	American Sunday.
Aug. 22, Tues.	Every Member-Friend Canvass.
Oct. 15, Sun.	Harvest Home Services.
Oct. 20, Fri.	Reception for Official Board.
Nov. 3, Fri.	Baseball Tournament.
Dec. 31, Sun.	Watch Night Services.

STAFF

Programs such as these are ambitious indeed. To assist in carrying out such programs about one-third of the forty churches employ besides the minister, an organist, a janitor and other paid workers. The churches at Buckhorn, Kentucky, and Sacaton, Arizona, are mission churches existing under exceptional conditions. Buckhorn's church plant includes a school, a hospital, an orphanage and a sawmill, so that the staff is large. For its work among the Indians of a large territory, the church at Sacaton has ten workers. The other eleven churches that have staffs vary in their procedure. Several have ordained assistants who serve as extension workers or care for outlying churches of a circuit while the pastor in charge devotes his attention to the church at the center and to executive duties. A number of the churches also employ women as deaconesses, parish visitors, or directors of religious education and of young people's activities. In two instances the staff is enlarged in summer when the roads are good and the more isolated neighborhoods are accessible. Some churches have physical directors or directors of recreation. The total number of staff workers exclusive of those at Buckhorn and Sacaton is twenty-three. Half of the churches that have staffs are without competition from any other recognized Protestant church.[2]

The average country church never dreams of engaging the time of any one except the minister. These successful churches, however, have taken on staffs made necessary by their work without financial difficulty, because their tasks are such as to meet general approval. In the light of their experience, it is impossible to resist calling attention to the fact that many small communities now receiving only the part-time services of a number of men, might revolutionize their religious and social life if they were to unite in one church and obtain high-grade professional leadership. At Collbran, Colorado, the Congregational church had for years barely managed to live. The larger program inaugurated in

[2] These figures on staff do not include workers supported on the foreign field.

1920 has more than justified support of a staff. Nor is this case exceptional among these churches. One of the greatest achievements of the churches with staffs is perhaps their winning of the church members so completely as to be able to utilize their loyalty and service in further expansion of the work.

Valuable as these staff workers have proved, two-thirds of the churches have achieved their success through the unaided efforts of pastor and members. They have shown skill in selecting and training volunteer leaders and workers. At Imperial, California, two former ministers, one of them from another community, have been persuaded to devote nearly all their leisure to the work of the church. In other places, other persons contribute, in volunteer labor, three working days each week. The work, moreover, has been so organized as to give maximum results for the time expended.

These churches have not yet evolved the ideal organization for the town and country church. Their numerous promising experiments indicate, however, that they are making progress. Already we can see several healthy tendencies at work. Some of the churches, especially those with departments, conceive the ideal system to be one in which the agencies all function as structural parts of the whole. Almost all try to enlist all their members in church work and to find for each a suitable specialized task. Moreover, the boards, the societies, the units or groups, and the committees or departments are not operating in the proud independence and isolation of two generations ago; on the contrary, efforts are being made in some cases to coördinate them, and to provide a representative cabinet as a unifying overhead body.

SUMMARY

Types of local church organizations are varied and changing. Among agencies that seem to be essential to the smooth functioning of the church as a whole are these:

Two official boards, one responsible for spiritual affairs, the other for material matters, but holding joint sessions at infrequent intervals.

A clearly defined field of service for each organization in the church.

Committees or departments to meet certain major needs uncared for by existing organizations.

A pastor's Cabinet or Council, on which serves one member from each official board and from each organization or major committee in the church, and which shall correlate all work, initiate plans and keep each organization informed as to the general policy and program.

Local leaders or groups in each neighborhood or block to care for immediate needs on behalf of the church, to welcome newcomers and to do personal work.

A thorough survey of the parish and community.

A parish map locating every home.

A definite program, setting goals for each year's work, adopted annually by the officers and congregation.

BIBLIOGRAPHY

Modern Church Management: A Study in Efficiency—ALBERT F. McGARRAH. Revell, 1917. 215 pp. $1.25.

Scientific Management in the Churches—SHAILER MATHEWS. University of Chicago Press, 1912. 66 pp. $.50.

A Modern Church Program: A Study in Efficiency—ALBERT F. McGARRAH. Revell. $.50.

The Study of a Rural Parish—RALPH A. FELTON. Missionary Education Movement, New York, 1914. $.50. Contains blanks for 99 homes and 38 pages of suggestions as to procedure and program.

Pastor's Manual of Survey and Program—WILLIAM L. BAILEY and CLARE JOHN HEWITT. Abingdon Press, New York, 1922. $5.00. Written from a Methodist point of view, but the most thoroughgoing manual of its kind and adaptable for any denomination.

TOPICS FOR DISCUSSION

1. a. "Christianity is essentially unorganized. When we organize it we destroy its chief charm. Organization . . . should be shunned by the Church." [1]

   b. "The more perfectly organized and managed is . . . the

[1] Babson, R. W., "The Future of the Churches," p. 103.

'church-temple,' the larger are the results which the in-dwelling Spirit can produce." [2]

Defend one of the opposed positions set forth in (a) and (b).

2. Beneath all differences in application, point out certain large tendencies pretty general in the organization of the forty successful churches.

3. "Theoretically the church should be regarded as a body of workmen ready to perform definite tasks as these tasks are outlined for them by its committee of management." [3]

Does the organization of the forty churches endeavor to put into practise the theory here set forth? If so, how?

4. Describe the organization of your own church. Is it such as to insure—

   (1) Service to the whole parish?
   (2) Adequate and progressive performance of all church functions?
   (3) Enlistment for service of every church member?
   (4) Avoidance of duplication in work of subordinate organizations?
   (5) Conflict of dates?

In what respects, when compared with the organization of the forty churches studied, is it capable of improvement?

5. Where a parish is divided into geographical groups or units with a leader for each, what offices within the districts may be given to boys and girls?

6. Among the handicaps of rural churches, President Butterfield includes the "boss system." [4] What does he mean? How may its organization insure a church against this danger?

7. What parts of the work of your church might well be under the supervision of departments? How many members would you appoint to each?

8. In your church, is there any waste effort as a result of the same thing being done by two agencies? E. g., does the Boy Scout Troop parallel an organized Sunday school class, or the Young Ladies' Society duplicate the work of the Ladies' Aid? How may such duplication be avoided?

[2] McGarrah, A. W., "Modern Church Management," p. 21.
[3] Mathews, Shailer, "Scientific Management in the Churches," p. 36.
[4] Butterfield, K. L., "The Country Church and the Rural Problem," p. 73.

9. In what circumstances is a four- or five-year program more effective than a program for one year? What is the danger in a cumulative series of objectives?

10. Prepare for your church a program for next year, following the arrangement used in either of the two programs given in this chapter.

Chapter VIII

PUBLICITY

From the dim past down to less than a century ago, organized religion obtained all the publicity it required through the peal of a bell. Now that life has become so complex, so crowded with distractions and duties, the church must compete for attention with many other interests. In this competition it has three objectives: to inform its own members and keep them interested in its life and work; to reach and capture persons not yet interested; and to permeate with its uplifting influences community life and standards.

To attain these three ends amidst the turmoil of the new day, it must have a definite and efficacious publicity program. Every one of the successful churches here studied has known this.

SLOGANS AND MOTTOES

Among simple devices, one of the most effective is a name or slogan. A certain open country church has assumed the rôle of "The Church of Community Interest." The Methodist church at Bingham Canyon, Utah, among the squalid surroundings of a rural industrial copper camp, dares to be known as "The Home of Happiness." Another congregation advertises itself as belonging to "a church with a purpose," the purpose being further emphasized by a seal which appears upon all printed matter issued by the church. "The Church on the Heights" has traded on its geographical location to suggest loftiness of spirit. Whatever the name or slogan adopted, these successful churches use it on every occasion. No printed matter, no newspaper article, appears without it. It becomes a synonym for the church, an embodiment of the idea for which the church stands.

church activities, and serve as a reminder to congregation and to friends that the church is at work and ready to serve.

These papers, with their comments on parish events, appeal to the general interest in events in which one has shared or in which one's acquaintances have figured. They also furnish a continuous record of the work of the church. The columns of the parish journal, moreover, can emphasize the great appeals of the Church at large. By way of "filler," the wise editor may employ thought-provoking epigrams and slogans.

The majority of these church papers are well edited. Their excellence of form is ascribed by some pastors to helpful suggestions from the local newspaper man. Most of the papers show good page arrangement, with clear-cut heads to articles and sufficient space between lines to attract the reader who might be repelled by a crowded page. The tone of a number of these organs may be characterized as breezy. The editors, whether they be pastors or laymen, have acquired the knack of what may be called snappy writing; of putting the important feature of the story well in the lead, and of rousing and holding the reader's interest. These papers are not issued merely for pastime, but because those who understand the labor of their production are convinced their publication is warranted by the results.

The expense of publishing them is met in various ways. Some are financed by means of commercial advertisements. Others are paid for, at least in part, by a small annual subscription price of from twenty-five to fifty cents. Occasionally the paper is published by the Christian Endeavor Society, the details of its business management being handled by the young people, with the pastor serving as editor-in-chief. In some instances the expense is borne by a publicity appropriation in the Church budget. A paper of this kind, as the local printer soon proves, is not expensive; a hundred dollars more or less represents the average outlay. These successful churches are convinced that sustained, energetic, live publicity brings in, either directly or indirectly, much more than it costs.

The problem of distribution is not serious. Generally the

paper is distributed at church, copies being mailed to those not in attendance. Sometimes the entire edition is mailed in advance of Sunday. In other cases the paper is distributed by the Boy Scouts; in still others several Sunday school classes attend to the distribution, each distributing an issue. The local church paper averages from four to eight pages, and is of a size that will enable it to be slipped into a large envelope, or when folded, into an envelope of ordinary size.

Some churches print instead of the parish newspaper, or in addition to it, an annual which contains a directory of the members and a program of activities, more or less detailed, for the year ahead. Some of these annuals, bound as attractive booklets, are meant to be preserved by the members for reference. The cost of publication is often paid for in part by advertisements. It is to be doubted whether an annual is as effective as a less ambitious parish newspaper appearing at more frequent intervals. An annual might be put out as one of the numbers of such a paper.

CALENDARS

A similar publicity device employed by several of the churches is an annual calendar carrying a picture of the church and containing reminders of the services and of the seasons of the church year. Through denominational publishing houses it is possible to obtain calendars of various sizes and designs, provided with blank spaces for the insertion of local matter.

Another form of printed publicity matter, which is used by the Methodist church of Rolla, Missouri, consists of cards with perforations at the top and the request, "Please hang me up in a conspicuous place." On one such card, below an attractive picture of the church, was a general invitation to a series of Sunday evening services. Toward the bottom were attached, calendar fashion, several uniform slips of paper, upon each of which, beside a portrait of the minister, was a detailed announcement of one of the services. Upon the card itself, hidden by the detachable slips, was a calendar of regular church activities.

MISCELLANEOUS ADVERTISING

These churches use the printing press in still other ways. Half of them employ at irregular intervals printed circulars announcing anything from a lawn party to the lenten services. More than half these churches also use large cards, placing them not only on their own bulletin boards but in the windows of various stores and at the hotels, the school and elsewhere.

THE MAIL SERVICE

Uncle Sam is a willing carrier, at a minimum of expense, of such advertisements as postal cards, folders, money-envelopes and letters. The publicity value of these is undeniable, especially in the country where the average person does not receive a large amount of mail. Virtually all the churches studied attribute great value to the personal letter. After an evangelistic campaign, in particular, the new member is glad to feel that the church is writing to him, proudly remembering his entry into the ranks and looking to him for coöperation and service. The minister of the Methodist Circuit at Larned, Kansas, sends to migrant harvest hands letters welcoming them as guests of the church and of the community during the season. The human and spiritual link established by mail with these homeless, friendless migrants is of incalculable value.

Letters, even when mimeographed or otherwise manifolded, enable the pastor to speak in a more direct and personal way than he can even in a parish paper. On a given subject a letter may be sent to members, a variant of it to friends of the church, another to men, and another to women or to young people. Postal cards are used, especially as announcements or reminders of coming events, by three-fourths of the churches. The Presbyterian church at Dayton, Indiana, keeps a special guest book in which visitors are asked to sign their names. Long after they have returned to their homes these visitors receive printed communications from the church.

GOOD TASTE AND STYLE

Writing of news is not made effective by exaggeration or by the piling up of adjectives, but by accuracy, crispness and naturalness. Conditions vary and so must style. The pastor who knows just what his church has to offer and just how much it means to the community, will know what to say. The pastor will know how to say it who knows the problems of the individuals and the families in his community. But the mechanics of advertising he usually has to study. From the local printer he should learn the beauty and the appropriate uses of the various fonts of type, the psychology of tasteful display methods, and the most effective uses of cuts. Failure properly to employ such mechanical devices results in expenditure of money without adequate return. Attention to details like these has gone far to render the publicity of the churches here studied unusually productive of results. The Church should not stoop, however, to vulgar advertising "stunts." Its publicity should be distinguished from the ordinary flood of advertisements by dignity and good taste.

THE TELEPHONE

Another common medium of publicity is the telephone, establishing as it does in a scattered rural community a personal and direct contact with church and pastor. The Methodist pastor at Lander, Pennsylvania, for example, with lieutenants on each of the five rural telephone lines, is able to spread rapidly throughout his community any church announcements.

PULPIT NOTICES

The obvious and time-honored method of spreading information through announcements from the pulpit has its value and still forms part of the publicity program in almost all churches. Surveyors were impressed, however, where this device was employed, with the brevity of the announcements. No time was lost over this part of the exercises. The minister had something to say; he said it and stopped.

In several communities so fortunate as to have but one church, announcements of church activities were made at various community gatherings; and in one case such notices were regularly given in each classroom of the consolidated school.

STEREOPTICON AND MOTION-PICTURES

Through its benevolences the local church takes part in the work of the Kingdom of God throughout the world. The scope of its publicity program, therefore, should also be world-wide. In this field of church publicity—which, of course, is more commonly known as missionary education— virtually all the successful churches make use of the stereopticon, or the moving-picture machine, or of both. Through these instruments, especially if care and taste are used in the choice of subjects and slides or films, both home and foreign missionary work can be vividly portrayed. The churches studied are unusually keen in ferreting out good sources of material. They draw not only upon the resources of their denominational boards, but where such service is rendered by the state university or state library, upon the many really beautiful lectures which these agencies put at their disposal at a very nominal cost.[1]

THE CHURCH MAGAZINE

Akin to this type of educational material are the national or regional periodicals of the denominations, which most of these churches recommend to their members in order to link them to the larger work of the denominational bodies. Subscriptions are obtained through the parish paper, pulpit announcements, and solicitation by one or another of the church societies. If the work is done by a society, this organization receives in some cases a considerable commission for its work.

[1] For further discussion of this topic see the chapters on Equipment and Missionary Education.

MANAGING AND PAYING FOR PUBLICITY

In four out of every five of these churches full responsibility for the publicity program rests with the pastor, who is, however, often assisted by individuals or by committees. For the rest of the churches, the matter is under the charge of a committee, or of an individual who sometimes is connected with the local paper.

The financing of the publicity program shows greater variety. In some churches the program is supported either by the proceeds of advertisements, by individual contributions or by a combination of the two methods. In three instances the pastor pays the bills, an indefensible procedure adopted only because these three churches are of the smaller, weaker, missionary type. One church sets aside for its publicity expenses the prayer meeting offerings for the year. In a few other instances, one or another of the organizations of the church pays the bills. In the majority of cases, however, a definite sum is written into the church budget, and against this appropriation the publicity expenses are charged. These sums range from $20 to $500, and average $121; and in the greater number of cases the amount is between $50 and $100. In some instances the appropriations named are over and above the receipts from advertisements and subscriptions. The churches all feel that the expense is more than justified. Only one church is reported to have reduced its appropriation; and even that one still applies $100 a year to publicity.

SUMMARY

The publicity program of an average town or country church should include several, and may include most, of the following methods and articles of equipment:

1. An inventory of the means at hand, as newspapers, movies, mail, telephone, other organizations, frequented centers including stores.
2. Connections with, and coöperation of editor, moving-picture theater proprietor, storekeepers, etc.

3. A church slogan or motto to be used in all articles, on stationery, etc.

4. A church seal. A die made from pen-and-ink drawing should not cost more than $2.00.

5. A typewriter for director of publicity. A machine of junior or portable type can be purchased for from $50 to $60.

6. A duplicator or mimeograph. Advertising pages of religious journals present various kinds, with prices. A duplicator may be had for about $10. Mimeographs come at various prices, the maximum price being $150.

7. One or more bulletin boards. A neat hand-made board for the posting of notices can be constructed for from $10 to $20. A manufactured board with movable letters ranges in price from $40 to $105.

8. A program of methods of publicity adopted, as parish paper, letters, etc., with frequency of each.

9. An organization, probably a publicity committee, with power to appoint a correspondent from each organization, an editor to check up on copy and prepare it for publication, a business manager to secure advertisements and subscriptions, to prepare and keep up-to-date mailing lists, and to arrange for distribution of all material published.

The above program includes many items. Not all need be used by any one church. Assuming there is a certain amount of equipment, the following is suggested as a maintenance budget for the year's publicity, adapted to a church of 150 members:

Paid advertising	$ 20.00
Window cards, leaflets and folders	30.00
Monthly letter to all members and friends (postage and stationery)	50.00
Stencils, typewriter ribbons, incidentals	7.50
Maintenance of bulletin boards, news letters, etc.	3.50
	$111.00

A four-page parish paper, costing from $8.00 to $10.00 per issue, can be made self-sustaining through advertisements and subscriptions.

BIBLIOGRAPHY

Church Advertising—W. B. ASHLEY. Lippincott, 1917. $1.50.
Church and Sunday School Publicity—HERBERT H. SMITH. Westminster Press, 1922. $1.25.
Handbook of Church Advertising—FRANCIS CASE. Abingdon Press, 1921. $1.25.

TOPICS FOR DISCUSSION

1. What should be the concrete objectives of a church's publicity?
2. What forms of publicity are best adapted to reach (a) non-church members; (b) church members rarely present at services; (c) regular attendants?
3. How may publicity be made a means not only of drawing people to services, lectures, etc., but of increasing the loyalty of members toward their church?
4. "The children of this world are in their generation wiser than the children of light." How true is this as applied to average methods of church and commercial advertising?
5. Outline publicity campaigns adapted to the following situations:

    (a) An open country church, alone in its community. Many non-members irregularly attend the services and other activities. Sum available for the year, $50.
    (b) A village community with two churches, both sparsely attended. A large Protestant factory element is untouched by local church influences. Sum available for the year, $150.

6. In what circumstances, if at all, should commercial advertisements appear on church publicity material?
7. How can church organizations such as the Boy Scouts be helpful in a campaign of publicity?
8. In conducting publicity for the church, against what dangers should we be on our guard?
9. How would you carry on an advertising campaign to increase interest in the mid-week service? What return can be expected from this type of announcement:

    "The minister and the janitor will hold their usual prayer meeting on Wednesday evening"?

10. What has your church to advertise? List in order of importance. Why should these attractions be advertised in the order you adopt? What proportion of time and money should be allotted to each of the various items?

Chapter IX

COMMUNITY WELFARE AND CHURCH COÖPERATION

The churches dealt with here have community service as an ideal. They show how a church can minister to the welfare of the community and how it can coöperate with other agencies that have kindred ideals, as well as with other churches. Much of the community service work of the churches has already been described. Their organizations do a great deal of it; their parish houses are community assets. Details already given will not be repeated in this chapter; but the more important facts will be summarized.

COMMUNITY WELFARE

I. COÖPERATION WITH THE SCHOOL

At Parma, Idaho, the church and schools coöperate at every point. Together they employ a man to take charge of music, who also leads all community singing. The school uses the community house gymnasium. The Superintendent of Schools is the adviser for the Senior Christian Endeavor Society, a large proportion of whose members are high school students. At Honey Creek, Wisconsin, the school, church and community house are regarded by the community almost as one plant, and the respective buildings are open alike to school, church and community for all reasonable purposes. The same situation exists in a number of other communities each of which has only one church. Many school auditoriums are open to the churches for lectures and entertainments. Three of the churches have lent the full weight of their influence to school consolidation campaigns, all of which have been successful. A number of ministers and of leading church members coöperate freely with parent-teacher associations. Several of the churches give annual receptions to the school teachers. One Sunday each year is also given to a discussion of the spiritual implications of education, and the relationship between the church and the school.

II. CIVIC IMPROVEMENT

(a) *Roads*—Good roads are vital to the country church, and the larger the parish the more important they are. There have been several instances of coöperation between church and community in behalf of good roads. The coöperative action at Collbran, Colorado, and Prairie Grove, Arkansas, may be taken as typical of these. The Collbran Congregational church held a special "Good Roads" meeting. After the exhibition of a moving-picture showing roads in the making, there was a discussion which led to immediate favorable action on the part of the citizens. At Prairie Grove, the Methodist church sent its Boy Scouts under the leadership of the pastor to help the business men who actually built a part of the Ozark Trail. Onlookers said that when the boys got to work "it was enough to make a steam shovel jealous."

(b) *Fire Department*—As described in Chapter IV, the Boy Scouts of Dayton, Indiana, under the leadership of the Presbyterian church, are also the town fire department. Their equipment includes a sixty gallon chemical engine, a few smaller chemical tanks, buckets, roof and extension ladders.

(c) *Law Enforcement*—These churches stand fearlessly for law enforcement. At Post Falls, Idaho, the pastor of the community church (Presbyterian) discovered that a good many of the townspeople, including the town marshal, were intoxicated at a lodge dance. He called a meeting for the next Sunday evening, at which the district judge and the prosecuting attorney were asked to speak, the pastor preaching on the topic—"The Disgrace of Post Falls." As a result the town marshal resigned, and the dance with booze is ended.

(d) *Politics*—The part of several of the men's organizations in insuring clean town government has already been discussed (see page 80).

(e) *Village Improvement*—Women's organizations in several churches have conducted campaigns for town improvement, have encouraged residents to plant flowers, furnished the community with playground equipment, beautified the railroad station, and campaigned for modern buildings along the main street and for modern appliances in the homes.

(f) *Poor Relief*—In several of the communities having only one church each, all poor relief efforts center in the church or in one of its subsidiary organizations.

(g) *Cultural Activities*—The concerts, lectures, lyceum courses and occasional Chautauquas promoted by these churches, are all of value to the community. A number of church buildings either house the community library or both house and manage it. To the small library of the church is added, in several of these, the traveling library of the state which was secured through the initiative of the pastor.

(h) *Citizenship Building*—All the character-building work of the church is citizenship building; but three of these churches have been peculiarly successful among special types of people, the Negroes, Mexicans, Indians. The Lone Oak—Montholia—Methodist circuit in Texas has restored to self-respect two discouraged Negro communities. Bank accounts have been started, farms purchased and educational activities carried on.[1] The Presbyterian mission at San Gabriel, California, has done a similar service for Mexicans. At Sacaton a mission, also conducted by the Presbyterians, has shown the fitness of the Indians for civilization and for Christianity.[2] To teach the Indians to value their land and to understand that debts incurred by the borrowing of money must be paid, the Mission maintains a loan fund. Through the influence of the Mission, a bank in a near-by town has also created such a fund.

(i) *Health*—The health work of these churches has been

[1] See "Churches of Distinction in Town and Country," Chapter VIII.
[2] Ibid., Chapter VII.

particularly significant. Two conduct medical clinics. One has both a medical clinic and a dental clinic which give service at very low rates. Clean-up week has been initiated in the communities of several. Hospitals at the county seat have been financially aided, and there has been active coöperation with the county Child Welfare organization and the Anti-tuberculosis Society. At Collbran, Colorado, there has been particularly effective coöperation with the board of health and the district nurse; while the exceptional church at Buckhorn, Kentucky, conducts its own small hospital with a resident staff of physicians and nurses. Health bulletins have been distributed. Pulpits have been opened occasionally to county health-nurses or officers of the state health department. A fearless, timely word by one pastor decided the citizens in favor of a much-needed sewerage project which did away with open cesspools that had long endangered the health of a prosperous village.

AGRICULTURAL WELFARE

These churches understand that it is not their business to preach scientific farming; but they do understand, as one pastor said, that—"If God's house is to prosper the soil must be kept fertile, the flocks and herds built up and the farm homes made contented and happy." Hence they have helped in many ways to improve methods and conditions of agriculture.

I. THE SURVEY

A survey of one church indicated that the economic condition of the community was not as serious as the people had believed it to be. The result was a revival of confidence and a new interest in crop diversification.

II. DEMONSTRATION FARM

Half a dozen of these churches have farms of their own. Several are used as actual demonstration points for the community. One pastor, a former county agent, bettered the whole life of a less favored agricultural community by showing how profits could be made by intensive cultivation and crop diversification. Two of the farms are the property of the Negro circuit just mentioned. The people share in the planting of the crops and divide the harvest from these farms. Agricultural clubs were formed and prizes awarded for the best specimens. Agricultural and canning clubs among the boys and girls are, in fact, quite common.

III. Farm Institutes, etc.

Ten of the churches have held farm institutes of one kind or another, bringing in specialists from the state department of agriculture and discussing topics of interest to the farmers and their communities. In two instances these institutes lasted for several days and there was a religious service each evening. In addition to the agricultural topics discussed at one of these institutes, the farm home, the community center, the school and religious training were given places on the program.

IV. Employment Service

Two churches operate a labor exchange or employment bureau, especially during the height of the harvest. In each instance there is no other agency to perform this service and the church has the personnel, the equipment and the office; more important still, it has the confidence of the community.

V. Agricultural Coöperation

Three churches have been directly or indirectly responsible for the organization of local units of the County Farm Bureau, or for the organization of the Grange. The influence of one church and its pastor caused membership of the town Chamber of Commerce to be opened to farmers. The problem of relationship between town and country forthwith disappeared.[3]

Naturally the church as a community institution co-operates with other institutions and agencies. Such co-operation has been indicated in the preceding paragraphs. The major service of a number of these churches has resulted, however, from their ability to organize the entire community for effective service, rather than from their co-operation with local agencies. Nevertheless, quite a number of the churches have been identified with the creation of community councils in which have centered virtually all community interests. Representation in the council is usually on an organizational basis, each lodge, and club, and school, and church having at least one delegate. The council functions through committees, each of which covers some phase of community interest, such as recreation, agriculture, home and school, health or civic improvement. This council serves as a clearing house for the organizations, prevents conflicts of dates, works out community programs upon which all can agree, and makes possible the settling of all the forces of the community in favor of an agreed-upon program with a minimum of lost effort and friction. In three instances the minister of the church is either president or secretary of this organization.

I. COÖPERATION WITH NATIONAL AGENCIES

A large number of these churches ally themselves definitely with certain national agencies, or with local branches of such agencies if these exist. Several give a room for the use of the Red Cross; many coöperate in the national membership drive of this organization. Representatives of the Near East Relief and similar agencies are given opportunity

[3] The service of the Larned, Kan., Methodist circuit to migrant laborers has been mentioned in this book and is also described in Chapter V of "Churches of Distinction in Town and Country."

to present their causes to the people. There is coöperation with the Y. M. C. A.; and two or three churches have classes organized as Y. M. C. A. groups. It should be said, however, that just because these churches are successful and are performing functions which in some communities fall to other agencies, there are instances in which they do not coöperate with outside organizations. In a number of cases the work for boys and girls is so well organized and so efficiently conducted that the churches have no need for the assistance of the Y. M. C. A. or the Y. W. C. A. They are doing everything that the Association would do for its boys; and in addition they are conducting activities for the other age- and sex-groups included in their membership.

II. INTERDENOMINATIONAL COÖPERATION

Naturally the agencies with which these churches ally themselves are most frequently religious. Ten of the forty, however, are in communities or neighborhoods where there are no other evangelical churches. The other thirty are very ready to coöperate. Such coöperation begins with union services, particularly on occasions of special interest to the nation or the community, such as Thanksgiving Day and Memorial Day or the Graduation Sunday of the high school. Union services in summer are common. In one instance there is a union Sunday school, and in another community the women's missionary societies of five churches have weekly prayer services. Coöperation in special evangelistic services is frequent, and union Christian Endeavor Society meetings are common. Churches with community houses frequently open them to sister denominations for special events, and the parish house of one contains a community kitchen which all can use. Plays or pageants staged by one or another of the organizations are frequently repeated throughout the area in which the church is known, for the benefit of causes in which nearby churches are interested. Teams of men, or of young folk, from the successful churches frequently go out to assist congregations or communities in which religious work or some department of

church organization seems to be languishing. Coöperation
in athletics has already been discussed.

These churches coöperate extensively in organized interdenominational activities. They are represented at church
and Sunday school conventions, and they make sure that
their delegates to such conferences report to them. Furthermore they give to interdominational agencies and causes.
Interdenominational coöperation is often directed by a ministerial association.

The extent to which these churches are willing to co-
operate with persons in other denominations is shown particularly by the ten which are the only churches in their communities. These ten all have associate or affiliated memberships which are open to adherents of other denominations
who do not desire to surrender their original connection,
but who do desire to worship in the community in which
they live. These affiliated members are admitted either upon
certification from their churches or on signing a simple confession of faith, acknowledging Jesus Christ as Savior and
promising to seek and obey His will. Under such conditions tolerance of one another's beliefs is imperative, and
this tolerance exists. At the Imperial, California, community church one Sunday evening the minister received
some members by sprinkling, some by immersion and some,
Friends, by a simple notice that they desired to unite with
the church. One elder, formerly a member of an immersion-
ist denomination, held the font while the minister performed
the rite of baptism by sprinkling; and another elder, a Friend,
who did not believe in any kind of baptism, helped to fill
the baptistry for the immersion. It will be seen, therefore,
why a number of these churches, though not Baptist in their
denominational affiliations, include the baptistry in their
equipment.

The results of this spirit of tolerance and coöperation are
clearly evident in the membership rolls. From a half-dozen
to sixteen denominations, including former Roman Catholics
and Mormons, are listed on the various membership rolls of
these churches.

These scattered instances are typical of many that have

been gleaned from the study of these churches. It is to be seen that they believe in teamwork. Where agencies exist that they can trust they are willing to depute certain tasks to them, and to coöperate to the full in the accomplishment of these tasks. On the other hand, where the need exists and other agencies are neither present nor within call, the church does not flinch from its responsibility to see that in every community there is an opportunity for a satisfying life, and where necessary the program is extended to meet the needs of the people.

BIBLIOGRAPHY

Fear God In Your Own Village—RICHARD MORSE. Holt, 1918. 212 pp. $1.30.

Church Coöperation in Community Life—PAUL L. VOGT. Abingdon Press, 1921. 171 pp. $1.00.

The Church at Play: A Manual for Directors of Social and Recreational Life—NORMAN E. RICHARDSON. Abingdon Press, 1922. 317 pp. $1.50.

TOPICS FOR DISCUSSION

1. "Bad politics, social evils, insanitary streets and houses, long hours for women workers, the labor of little children, rotten municipal administrations will continue as long as churches continue to regard themselves as rival groups without social functions. They will be to a large extent mitigated, if not in many cases destroyed, if the churches of any community deliberately undertake the process of evangelizing public opinion."[4] Show how some church or group of churches has improved each kind of bad conditions named.

2. What levers has the country church by which to influence public opinion?

3. Express in writing your conception of the phrase "social gospel." Do you accept the ideal it sets for the church?

4. Check any of the following that are needed in your community: improved roads, farmers' coöperative organization, public waterworks, hospital, sewers, inspection of milk,

[4] Mathews, Shailer, "Scientific Management in the Churches," pp. 49, 50.

campaign against flies or mosquitoes, laws about wells, laws about sanitation, about quarantine against contagious diseases, garbage collection, clean-up day, telephone, hall for public gatherings, lecture course. What has your church done to help bring about any such improvement?

5. What conditions in your community are worrying conscientious parents? (E.g., jazz dancing, hooch, objectionable movies, rowdyism among young people, a pool-room or other place of resort where influences are bad, etc.) In regard to each live issue, tell what your church is actually doing to meet the situation, and what more it might do.

6. Has a church anything to do with running water in farm kitchens? If so, what? Mention three ways in which a community church can raise the standard of living in the community.

7. What do people talk about in your community? Listen to the conversation at the country store, the moving-picture theater, the church steps, between church and Sunday school, the Ladies' Aid, jotting down topics. What proportion of time is given to (1) people, (2) things, (3) ideas? How much time is consumed in superficial or malicious gossip? How much interest is indicated by the talk in the program of the church?

8. "Nothing to do in the country." Show how this complaint may afford the country church (1) an opportunity, (2) a challenge.

9. What is the practical reason why country churches should concern themselves with agricultural prosperity?

10. To what extent did religion among the ancient Hebrews concern itself with agriculture? Cite illustrative passages.

11. In what circumstances should calf or canning clubs be conducted in connection with a church?

12. From this chapter and from "Country Churches of Distinction," draw varied illustrations of the coöperation of churches with the Farm Bureau.

13. For a village community of 800 to 1,200 people in a Protestant district where there is no marked separation between racial, occupational or social groups, and where sectarian differences are not strong, which of the following should be the minister's objective? Support your choice.

   (a) Two churches working in coöperation.
   (b) A single denominational church.
   (c) A single federated church.

14. Give accounts of specific cases where the influence of a church through its members has accomplished indirectly definite service for the community.

15. Ought it to be the ideal that the church members should do welfare work solely through their church? Or should organizations specialized for certain forms of service be deputed to perform it, the churches coöperating either as such or through individual members?

16. A minister goes into a town where there are a Business Men's Club, a Parent-Teacher Association, a Commercial Club and three Protestant churches besides his own, all these organizations working independently for what each considers the good of the community. Should the minister take steps to bring about coöperation? What can he do?

17. Describe how some church known to you has lessened its own organized activities in order to promote Christian coöperation more broadly conceived.

18. To what extent, if any, does a church by coöperating with such an agency as, for example, the Anti-Saloon League, vouch for that agency's good faith?

Chapter X

MEASURING SUCCESS

Reasons for the success of these churches were eagerly
sought. The testimony of the local people is interesting on
this point. Of the explanations they gave, the three that
seemed most important to the field worker have been selected.
For the forty churches, therefore, there are 120 possible
answers. In twenty-one instances the pastor receives credit.
In fifteen cases, success is accounted for by the all-round
program; in thirteen, by coöperation with other churches
and the community agencies. In nine cases the young
people receive credit, and in eight the recreational program.
In eight other instances the high quality and general level
of intelligence of the people themselves more than anything
else seemed to account for the success of the church. Long
pastorates are mentioned in seven instances; the economic
program of the church in four. The minister's wife and
local lay leadership of the church also came in for their
share of the recognition in four cases each. The remaining
explanations cover such items as equipment, men's organizations, publicity, and the annual survey.

THE PAR STANDARD

During the Interchurch World Movement much was made
of a so-called Par Standard for town and country churches,
which sought to set down those items of equipment and program believed to be within the reach of any rural church.
No attempt was made to appraise the various items of this
standard; but it was divided under the five heads of Equipment, Pastor and Services, Finance, Religious Education,
Community Service and Coöperation. This standard con-

tained thirty points, only twenty-four of which were covered in the schedules used by the Interchurch World Movement. On the basis of the forty churches, a new standard has been worked out, one that is probably above par, but which does summarize the principal items of equipment and program which these churches have in common.

In this standard, no item has been included unless at least 20 per cent. of the churches qualified. Furthermore, an attempt has been made to avoid carrying classification to too fine a point. Thus, while fourteen of these churches have gymnasiums, a gymnasium as such was not included in the standard. Instead, the church was graded on the basis of having a space available for social and recreational purposes which might or might not be in a gymnasium or separate community house.

This summary of equipment and program follows; and for each item is given the number of churches of the forty which have made this particular point. The points that are starred are those in the original studies on which the Interchurch World Movement gathered data. At the conclusion of the table will be found a comparison of the ranking of the churches in the twenty-five typical counties studied by the Committee [1] with the ranking of these forty churches.

PAR STANDARD

PHYSICAL EQUIPMENT

* 1. A comfortable, attractive parsonage with modern improvements, furnished rent free................ 33
* 2. Auditorium with seating capacity adequate to maximum attendance at regular services.............. 34
  3. Pipe organ or piano........................... 40
* 4. Space for social and recreational purposes fitted with movable chairs and a platform, and large enough for the largest crowds in the habit of assembling there.... 35
* 5. Separate rooms or curtained spaces for Sunday school classes or departments.................... 32
* 6. Moving-picture machine or stereopticon facilities... 28
  7. A well-planned, well-equipped kitchen............ 34

[1] Town and Country Series, in 12 volumes, by the Committee on Social and Religious Surveys.

8. Sanitary lavatories............................ 26
* 9. Parking space for automobiles or horsesheds...... 39
*10. All property kept in good repair and sightly con-
     dition 35
11. Bulletin boards for display of church announce-
    ments 25
12. Playground 12
13. Recreational equipment—games, volley ball, cro-
    quet, quoits (indoor and outdoor) and the like.... 28

RELIGIOUS AND MISSIONARY EDUCATION

*14. Sunday school maintained throughout the year.... 40
*15. Sunday school enrollment at least equal to church
     membership, with an average attendance of at least
     two-thirds of its membership..................... 20
*16. Definite and regular attempt to bring pupils into
     church membership, and specific instruction in
     preparation therefor............................. 40
*17. Teacher training or normal class regularly provided 20
*18. Definite provision for enlistment and training of
     leaders for church and community work other than
     in Sunday school................................. 27
*19. Communicant classes regularly held in preparation
     for church membership.......................... 23
20. Week-day religious instruction provided.......... 10
21. Daily Vacation Bible School held................ 11
22. School of Missions, or systematic Mission Study
    class regularly held............................. 8
23. The missionary work of the church regularly pre-
    sented from the pulpit and in the Sunday school.... 33
24. At least one representative in professional Christian
    service during the last ten years.................. 19

FINANCE

*25. The church budget, including both local expenses
     and benevolences, adopted annually by the congre-
     gation 40
*26. Every-member canvass for weekly offerings made
     annually on the basis of the local and benevolent
     budget adopted; all church members and adherents
     canvassed; envelope system used.................. 36
*27. The budget of benevolence either meeting the de-
     nominational apportionment in full or equal to one-

third of the current expense budget (Interchurch
standard 25 per cent.)........................... 13

28. All current bills paid monthly 39

29. A systematic plan of payments on principal and interest of debt on the church property, if any....... 18

30. Property insured................................. 38

PASTOR

*31. A pastor resident within the bounds of the com-
munity 40

*32. A pastor giving full time to the work of this church 33

*33. The pastor receiving a total salary of at least \$1,500
a year and free use of house (Interchurch figure
\$1,200) 34

PROGRAM

*34. At least one service of worship every Sunday..... 40

35. Regular mid-week services....................... 24

*36. Church works systematically to extend its parish to
the limits of the community...................... 40

37. Church works systematically to serve all occupational classes in the community and all racial elements which do not have their own Protestant
churches 35

38. A definite program setting goals for the year's work
adopted annually by the officers and congregation
and held steadily before the attention of the church. 18

39. A definite assumption of responsibility with respect
to some part of this program (as in 38) by at least
25 per cent. of the active members............... 37

40. Systematic evangelism aimed to reach the entire
community and every class in the community...... 40

41. A minimum net membership increase of 10 per cent.
each year....................................... 20

42. Community service a definite part of the church's
work, including a definite program of community
coöperation led by or participated in by the church. 40

*43. Definite organized activities for all the various age-
and sex-groups in the congregation and community
(as in Young People's Society, Men's Brotherhood,
Boy Scouts, or similar efforts)................... 24

44. A systematic and cumulative survey of the parish
with a view to determining the church relationships
and religious needs of every family, and such a

mapping of the parish as will show the relationships
of each family to local religious institutions together
with a continuous and cumulative study of the social,
moral and economic forces of the community with a
view to constant adaptation of program to need.... 16

COÖPERATION

*45. Coöperation with other churches of the community
in a definite program for community betterment[2]... 31
46. Coöperation with state and county interdenominational religious agencies......................... 40
47. Coöperation with local community organizations.... 38
48. Coöperation with county, state, or national welfare
agencies 38
49. Coöperation with local and county agricultural
agencies 36
50. Coöperation with denominational boards.......... 40

A comparison of the ranking of the successful churches
and those in the twenty-five counties, to which allusion has
frequently been made, covering only those points found in
the Interchurch World Movement schedules, shows that these
churches rank more than twice as high as those in the twenty-
five counties. The proportion of points attained is 85.5 per
cent. in the one case and 40 per cent. in the other. In those
points relating to the minister and worship, finance, and
religious education, the successful churches better the records
of the average from 100 to 150 per cent. The nearest approach in the two groups is in the matter of physical equipment where the superiority is a little less than 70 per cent.

This comparison shows only what is to be expected. If
these churches did not markedly exceed the average they
would not be successful. That they do exceed the average
simply proves that they are worthy to be studied and their
methods to be adapted. The most significant difference
disclosed by the comparison relates to community service and
coöperation. It is in this very important branch of church
work that the greatest difference is discernible, one of about
400 per cent.

One of the most interesting things which this survey

[2] Nine churches are the only ones in their respective communities.

reveals is the similarity in program between town, village, and country churches. The extent to which the town churches reach the outlying rural population has already been pointed out. The experiences of these churches prove that the town and the country to a remarkable degree respond alike to the same kind of organized expression of religion.

This investigation, particularly summarized as it is in the above standard, indicates very clearly that the rural church is now in possession of a program that meets the needs of the people. There is no occasion to flounder. There need be no hesitancy in leadership. The dream of a church that would stand central in the life and thought of its community has become an actuality, in these instances and in others equally significant.

The Country Church was challenged a dozen years ago to rise to the full possibility of its powers. The challenge came in the unimpassioned findings of a government report, that made by the Roosevelt Country Life Commission. These forty churches and the ideas and the ideals which they have formulated are the answer to that challenge. They prove that evangelistic zeal and social service can be combined under adequate leadership in a program that will rouse the interest and then command the loyalty of a community of any kind in country or in town.

Index

Advertising, miscellaneous, 147
Agriculture, 70
Agricultural coöperation, 158
Agricultural welfare, 157
Amount of expenditures, 116
Apportionment of expenditures, 116
Assessments, 113
Athletics, 67
Attendance, 48
Auditorium, the, 90

Baseball league, 67
Basement, the, 91
Bible study for public school credit, 50
Bibliography, 36, 44, 61, 86, 106, 121, 137, 152, 162
Boy Scouts, 66
Boys and girls, nurturing, 33
organizations for, 66
Budget, 109
Bulletin boards, 141

Calendars, 146
Campaign publicity, 110
Camping, 68
Canvass, every-member, 109, 112
Centerton, church building at, 104
Character reading, 70
Children, 72
worship for, 40
Church,
external appearance, 89
definite building plans, 99
other details of building, 94
plans for, 100-103
service for the, 75, 78
Church calendar, 133
Church membership, classes to prepare for, 31
Church press, 144
Church program, 123, 129
four year program, 132
unified, for 1922-1923, 131

Circuit evangelism, 33
Citizenship building, 156
Civic improvement, 155
Civic righteousness, 80
Classes, 50
Clubroom, the, 71
Coasting, 68
Collbran, church building at, 105
Collections, 71
Community house, 95
Community organization, 159
Community service, 76, 79
space and equipment for, 92
Community welfare, 154
Comparative results, 35
Conferences, 76
Cradle roll, 49
Curriculum, 50
Cultural activities, 156

Daily vacation bible school, 54
Debts, 117
Decision day, 53
Demonstration farm, 157
Denominational campaigns, 115
Discussion, topics for, 44, 61, 87, 106, 121, 137, 152, 162

Educational activities, 70
Employment service, 158
Enrollment, 55
Equipment for religious education, 47
Evangelistic harvest, preparation for, 26
Evening service, Sunday, 40
Extension evangelism, 34
Extra-curriculum activities, 52

Farm institutes, etc., 157
"Father and Son" banquet, 77
Finance, 109
Financial methods, other, 113
Financing the Sunday school, 119
Fire department, the, 155

Follow-up, the, 116
Forum, 41
Four-year program, the, 132

Girl Scouts, 66
Girls and boys,
    nurturing, 33
    organizations for, 66
Good taste in writing church
    news, 148
Graded lessons, 50
Gymnasium, 95

Health, 156
Home department, 49
Home mission aid, 118
Hiking, 68

Indians, set the pace, 33
Interchurch World Movement
    schedules, 169
Interdenominational coöperation,
    54, 160

Junior Christian Endeavor, 72

Kitchen, the, 92

Larger religious service, 78
Law enforcement, 155
Leadership, 55, 75
Leadership training, 59
Lessons, graded, 50
Life service recruits, 58

Magazine, the church, 149
Mail service, 147
Meetings, 77
    evangelistic, 30
Membership,
    enlisting the, 26
    using the, 41
Men, societies for, 77
Methods, other evangelistic, 30
Mid-week service, 42
Mission study outside the church
    school, 56
Missionary education, 56
    other methods of, 57
Missions,
    and women, 82
    at home, 83
    topics for discussion on, 64

Morning service, 39
Mottoes, 140
Motion-picture publicity, 149
Moving-pictures, 41, 97
    cost of, 97
    program, 97-98
    sources of films, 98
    topics of discussion on, 108,
        112
Music, 39

National agencies, coöperation,
    159
Non-evangelical pupils, 47
Nurseries, 81

Opportunities, meeting unusual,
    76
Organization, 49

Par standard, the, 165-169
Parish map, 129
Parish service, enlisting for, 58
Parish visiting, 81
Parma, church building and com-
    munity house at, 105
Pastor's council, 126
Per capita expenditure, 114
Politics, 156
Poor relief, 156
Prayer meetings, 27
Preparatory steps, 28
Press, the, 142
Printing-press, a, 144
Program, value of a full, 76
Promotion day, 53
Prospects, letters to, 29
Public "movie," 144
Publicity, 28, 110, 140
    managing and paying for, 150
Pulpit notices, 148
Pupils, 47

Radio, 71
Rally day, 52
Reaching an entire community,
    79
Records, 129
Recreational activities, 66, 70
Relief of poor, 156
Restroom, a, 83

Results,
  comparative, 35
  following up, 32
Roads, 155
Rodeo, 68

Schools, of missions, 57
Sermons, 39, 40
Service, 72
Service for the church, 75, 78
  larger religious service, 78
Services, 38
Similarity in program of town,
    village and county churches,
    170
Slogans, 140
Social activities, 66, 70, 73
Social occasions, 54
Societies for men, 77
Societies for women, 80
Speakers, addresses by invited,
    41
Special days, 31
Special offerings, 115
Staff, 135
Stage, the, 93
Stereopticon—publicity, 149
Stereopticons, 96
Stewardship day, 53
Stewardship training, 119
Style, in writing church news,
    148

Success, measuring, 165
Sunday school, providing for, 90
Survey of the church, 128, 157

Taking shut-ins to services, 82
Teachers and their preparation,
    51
Telephone, the, 148
Terms, 55
Tithing, 114
Training classes, 51

Unified church program for
    1922-1923, 131

Village improvement, 156
Vocational training, 69
Volunteer day, 59

Welfare, community, 154
Women,
  and missions, 82
  societies for, 80
Workers conference, 52
Workers, training personal, 27
Worship, 38
  for children, 40

Young people's organizations, 73

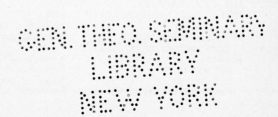

THIS BOOK

Should Be Read in Connection
with Its Companion Volume

CHURCHES OF DISTINCTION
IN TOWN AND COUNTRY

In which are Told
The Life-stories of Fourteen of the Forty
Successful Churches whose Methods have
been Treated Topically in the foregoing
pages. Each story constitutes in itself
A ROMANCE OF PASTORAL SUCCESS

Published by GEORGE H. DORAN COMPANY, New York

FOR

THE COMMITTEE ON SOCIAL AND RELIGIOUS
SURVEYS

370 SEVENTH AVENUE, NEW YORK

Freely Illustrated   *12mo. Net, $1.50*